SCHOOL CHOICE

SCHOOL CHOICE

Why You Need It — How You Get It

David Harmer

CATO INSTITUTE
Washington, D.C.

Library of Congress Cataloging-in-Publication Data

Harmer, David, 1962–
    School choice : why we need it, how we get it / David Harmer.
      p.   cm.
    Includes bibliographical references and index.
    ISBN 1-882577-14-0 : $22.95 — ISBN 1-882577-15-9 : $12.95
    1. School choice—United States.   2. School choice—California
  3. Educational vouchers—Law and legislation—United States.
  4. Educational vouchers—Law and legislation—California.   I. Title.
LB1027.9.H37 1994
371′.01—dc20   94-30046
                                                            CIP

Cover Design by Colin Moore.

Printed in the United States of America.

CATO INSTITUTE
1000 Massachusetts Ave., N.W.
Washington, D.C. 20001

To My Father,
John L. Harmer

Contents

Preface

On November 2, 1993, the Parental Choice in Education Initiative appeared on California's statewide ballot as Proposition 174. Although defeated, this initiative focused renewed attention on the persistently poor performance of the public schools and the need for alternatives to them. Proposition 174 is already serving as a model for school choice efforts in other states. This book, which contains the full text of the initiative and a thorough explanation of issues surrounding it, should be a useful guide to proponents of such efforts.

The book had its genesis in the heat of the drive to qualify the initiative for the ballot. Late in 1991 I left my law firm to serve as president of the Excellence Through Choice in Education League (ExCEL). For the better part of the following year I was the initiative's full-time advocate, promoting it in public speeches, on radio talk shows, and in televised debates throughout the state. During these appearances I found myself answering the same questions repeatedly and assuaging the same fears. It became apparent that existing materials did not adequately explain the need for school choice or answer the arguments against it. Even our supporters lacked the information they needed to be effective advocates.

This book attempts to fill that void.

Every child deserves the benefits that come through school choice. I hope this book will help persuade legislators and voters to make those benefits available.

—David J. Harmer
May 3, 1994

Author's Notes

My analysis of the condition of public education draws on evidence and examples from throughout the nation. Whenever possible, however, I illustrate my points with personal experience. In doing so, of necessity I discuss events and circumstances in California, particularly in the Los Angeles Unified School District (LAUSD). Since I resided within LAUSD boundaries during my tenure as president of ExCEL, it is the district with which I am most familiar. Some might argue that LAUSD, as a massive and deeply troubled urban district, is atypical. Perhaps so, yet its fundamental problems, both exogenous (rising violence, declining family stability) and structural (unwieldy bureaucracy, cumbersome regulation), are shared by most public school systems nationwide.

* * *

Schools are usually categorized as either "public" or "private." This book instead categorizes them as "government" or "independent."

"Public" schools are operated by governmental entities. Funded through compulsory taxation, they charge no tuition. Thus any student, regardless of economic status, may attend. "Private" schools, in contrast, are operated by nongovernmental entities. Lacking the guaranteed tax revenues of the "public" schools, they must charge tuition. Thus, as a rule, only students from families able to make the necessary financial sacrifice may attend.

Under school choice these distinctions blur, and the usual labels become misleading. School choice levels the playing field. All students would be eligible to receive tuition vouchers worth a certain percentage of the per-pupil cost of "public" schooling. They could then redeem the vouchers at any qualified school. Ideally, "public" schools would be funded only to the extent that parents voluntarily chose to enroll their children there, and "private" schools could accept tax-funded vouchers, thus enabling more low- and middle-income students to enroll. In short, "public" schools would need to compete more like "private" schools, and "private" schools could be funded more like "public" schools.

For the sake of clarity, this book identifies any school operated by a traditional governmental entity as a "government" school. All other schools are identified as "independent" schools, regardless of the ultimate sources of their funding. These terms apply under the present system and under school choice with equal accuracy.

* * *

References to government schools should be understood as including all kindergarten through 12th grade education funded and operated by the state and its subdivisions. References to government schools exclude higher education unless otherwise noted. References to independent schools should be understood as including all non-government kindergarten through 12th grade schools. Home schools may or may not be included, depending on the context. Average independent school tuition calculations generally exclude home school students, who would bring the average even lower. Overall independent school enrollment calculations generally include home school students.

PART I

THE NEED FOR SCHOOL CHOICE

Introduction:
The Greatest Force

I grew up in pleasant suburbs, but from 1990 through 1992 I belonged to an inner-city church. It was an education. Located a block from the intersection of Western Avenue and Pico Boulevard in Los Angeles, our building rarely survived a week without being defaced by spray-painted graffiti. After the Rodney King riots the neighborhood looked like a Third World war zone, but frankly it didn't look much better before. Our congregation was racially mixed, mostly poor, and full of the warmest and finest in human nature. Outside of my own family I have never met more loving people. For two years they were my neighbors. They will always be my friends.

While living in central Los Angeles I spent a night or two every week doing volunteer work, which took me into the homes of church members and their neighbors. I met Chuck and Tammy Woodhouse, who paid $1,900 a year to send their daughter to a Catholic school. They weren't Catholic, but their little girl was safe there, and she was actually learning. They couldn't be sure of either in the government school.

Many other parents I met desperately wanted to do what Chuck and Tammy had done; they wanted to send their children to better, safer schools. But they couldn't afford them.

Several black pastors in the area were so dismayed by the dismal quality of government schools in their neighborhoods that they were establishing bare-bones independent schools through their churches. Fundraising is a struggle anywhere, but imagine trying to do it in south central Los Angeles. They undertook this almost impossible task because they wanted their kids to be safe, cared for, and taught.

May I share the story of one former pastor I came to know? We met on January 9, 1992, in his office in a converted warehouse in Lynwood, a blighted area south of Los Angeles near Watts.

3

* * *

"Welcome, Mr. Harmer! How are you?" Reverend Matthew R. Harris, executive director of Project Impact, pumped my arm and brought me into his office. Beaming with pride, he showed me pictures and plaques as we got acquainted.

"Tell me your story," I said. "What is Project Impact? How did you come to be involved with it?"

"I got tired of conducting funerals for 15-year-olds," he answered. "I wanted to reach them on the streets before any more came to me in a coffin."

So Matt Harris left his pastorate to found Project Impact, a juvenile diversion agency serving the poorest areas of Los Angeles County. His purpose was to help adolescents in serious trouble—victims of drug, alcohol, and physical abuse, premature pregnancy, and broken homes, usually referred to him from the juvenile courts or expelled from the government schools, which takes some doing. "They are traumatized," Harris said. "Alienated." But with love and hard work they could be helped. He had rehabilitated a good number of them. Once rehabilitated, though, many of them had to return to dysfunctional schools, "where it's legal to pass out condoms and illegal to pass out Bibles. Is it any wonder we have a problem?"

I asked Harris why the government school system was unable to meet the needs of these youths. "Number one," he replied,

> you do not take a person who for years has been hobbled by chains of poverty, neglect, discrimination, and substandard education, bring him up to the starting line of a race, turn him loose on an uneven field, and say, "You're free to compete." It's not enough to open the gates of opportunity. We must nurture our youths' ability to walk through those gates.
>
> To do that, the roots of education have to go deeper. We need to reduce drug abuse and violence; we need to raise discipline and competence. That takes knowledgeable teachers, strong moral leadership, an emphasis on traditional subjects, a clear mission, an orderly and quiet learning environment, frequent monitoring of student progress, parental support, and strict standards. If a school fails to use these building blocks, no amount of money or busing or special programs will produce results.

"That seems obvious," I observed. "Are you saying the schools don't do that?"

4

A lot of public schools, especially the ones serving our black and Hispanic population, have fallen away from these practices. The conscientious student is severely penalized in such schools. As the system now operates, he has no alternative. Poor parents who want something better can't afford private school tuition. What are they supposed to do? Keep their kids in violent schools? Let them drop out?

In this area, 40 to 50 percent of our youth are dropping out, and when they stay in, 89 percent of the seniors score below the 50th percentile and only 6 percent go on to college. About 65 percent are unemployed. Education is the first rung up the economic ladder, but for us that rung is broken.

Noting the state's huge budget deficit and the struggles of many school districts, I asked what the state and its schools could realistically do. "They can give us choice," Harris said.

We don't need more money; there's already money in the system. We just need the power to determine where it's spent. Poor parents need consumer power. Let them choose schools that reflect the values they're trying to teach at home. More and more of them would opt for a private school if they could afford it. If the good schools could attract students *and funding* away from the bad ones, the bad ones would get motivated right away. They would have to work harder and smarter.

I asked Harris whether he would consider starting a school. "I would be running an alternative learning center for troubled kids right now," he replied, "if only I could get half what we spend per student in the public schools. I could be helping a lot of kids."

* * *

Contrast Matt Harris with Mark Slavkin, a member of the Los Angeles Board of Education. On August 19, 1992, Slavkin and I debated the Parental Choice in Education Initiative on a local television station's public affairs program. During a break, I told him, "I'm going out to put some coins in the parking meter. Can I get yours?"

"Oh, I don't need to worry about it," he said.

"Why?" I asked. "I thought the whole street had a one-hour limit."

"The school board oversees a budget of $3.9 billion," he answered. "That's bigger than some states. We don't have time to worry about parking meters. We have official license plates that let us park anywhere." Then he smiled and said, "The perks of power."

* * *

Which of these two will do the better job of educating children? To whom would you rather entrust your own child? Under the present system, Slavkin and his fellow politicians get your children and your tax dollars regardless of the performance of the schools they manage. School choice would give Matt Harris and others like him the freedom to compete, the opportunity to do a better job for less.

California's public school system costs the taxpayers over $5,200 per student per year. Chuck and Tammy Woodhouse found a preferable independent school for only $1,900 a year. Their neighbors wanted to make the same choice but lacked the means to do so. Isn't something wrong with this picture? The state is forcing parents to consume $5,200 in tax money by sending their children to government schools when for less than half that amount, if only given the freedom to do so, they could send their children to schools that work better.

Why not take a portion of the tax money required to keep a child in the government school system and give parents the option of using it to send the child to an independent school instead? It wouldn't cost the parents anything. It wouldn't cost the taxpayers anything; in fact, they would save money. The children would be safer and happier and could learn more. All parties (except possibly the government school employee unions) would come out ahead.

That is the essence of school choice. It offers every child the opportunity for a better education by offering parents the freedom and the funding to choose the school that best meets their children's needs. This is a simple, fair idea whose time has come. If the love of liberty can open the Iron Curtain, surely it can open the government school system to healthy competition.

The greatest force in the world is love. School choice unleashes that force. Most parents love their children more than anyone and anything else. My experience in the inner city showed me that parents in the poorest circumstances sometimes have the strongest desire for their children to do better. They want good schools and they know where good schools are.

School choice opens those schools to them . . . and to all of us.

1. What Are Schools For?

One summer day at a neighborhood picnic in our local park, my friend Chris Matthews and I were visiting. He had heard of my work on California's Parental Choice in Education Initiative and wanted to talk about it, so we went over to an open picnic table and sat down. Chris has five kids, the kind that make you hope your own turn out so well. He wants the best possible education for them, and he was intrigued by the initiative. He liked the idea of letting parents choose the best school for their kids, rather than simply send them where the district says. He also liked the $2,600 scholarship—half the annual cost to the taxpayers of providing a government school education—that would make an independent school a realistic option for most students. But he had one big concern.

"Dave, what will your initiative do to the public school system?"

I've heard that question countless times. In fact, almost every time I speak in favor of school choice, someone asks the same question: "What will your initiative do to the public schools?"

I ask in reply a more fundamental question: "What will it do for the education of our children?"

What school choice does to any government school system depends chiefly on that system's willingness to provide quality education. School choice doesn't focus on the needs of the system; it focuses on the needs of the children the system is supposed to serve. As former secretary of education Bill Bennett has observed, schools don't exist to exist; they exist to teach.[1] Maintaining a system isn't our goal; teaching children is. The government school system is a means to that end, not an end in itself. Failure to make that distinction distorts most discussions of educational reform, which tend to center on how to shore up the present system rather than how to teach children.

[1] William J. Bennett, "An Obligation to Educate," *California Political Review*, Summer 1992, pp. 20, 36.

The government school system merits respect, if any, not for what it is, but for what it does. Let us, then, ask two questions:

1. What should schools do?
2. Are the government schools doing it?

What should schools do? Entire books consider the question,[2] and for the education establishment the answers are many and complex. So pervasive is the confusion concerning the mission of schools, observes Jeremy Rabkin, that "the government has become preoccupied with ever more ambitious programs for multicultural recognition and bilingual education while public schools can no longer assure that even native English-speakers will learn to read and write and do arithmetic at what were once grade-school levels."[3]

What should schools do? For parents the answer is simple: Teach the basics! At the very least parents expect schools to teach reading, writing, and arithmetic. On this there is virtually universal agreement. They also expect schools to teach other academic subjects: history, geography, the sciences. In the process, most parents want schools to reinforce the common values of a free republic, such as respect for the life, liberty, property, and opinions of others.

Through their substantial tax burden these parents are paying *for* the schools, and they are clear about what they want *from* the schools: the teaching of the academic basics. They want schools to prepare students for productive work, for higher education, and for responsible citizenship.

Judged against these expectations, the government school system is failing.

---

[2] A praiseworthy example is John Goodlad, *What Schools Are For* (Bloomington, Ind.: Phi Delta Kappa Educational Foundation, 1979).

[3] Jeremy Rabkin, quoted in "Other Comments," *Forbes*, April 25, 1994, p. 28.

2. Government School Performance

How are the government schools performing? Just look. People are voting with their feet. A recent cover of *U.S. News & World Report* says it all: "The Flight From Public Schools." "Many parents," the article begins, "view the public schools as ineffective and dangerous, and are exploring other options before it's too late."[1] How many parents? In some states, most of them. A 1991 survey of 800 registered California voters found that over 50 percent of them felt that their local government schools were doing a poor job, and 70 percent believed that government schools statewide were doing a poor job. Dissatisfaction was highest among Hispanic and African-American voters.[2]

Their dissatisfaction is amply justified. In fact, "poor" may be too generous an assessment of government school performance. "The educational foundations of our society are presently being eroded by a rising tide of mediocrity that threatens our very future as a Nation and a people," warned the National Commission on Excellence in Education in its watershed report, *A Nation at Risk*.[3] Reviewing the conditions causing such alarm, John Chubb and Terry Moe of the Brookings Institution found that "not only were SAT [Scholastic Aptitude Test] scores declining year by year, but American students consistently did worse, often dramatically and embarrassingly worse, than foreign students on internationally standardized tests, particularly in the areas—math and science—so crucial to technological sophistication."[4]

[1]"The Flight from Public Schools," *U.S. News & World Report*, December 9, 1991, cover and p. 66.

[2]Arnold Steinberg and Anna David, "Summary Report: Survey of Voter Attitudes in California toward a Choice System in Education," Reason Foundation Policy Insight no. 130, October 1991, pp. 1–2.

[3]National Commission on Excellence in Education, *A Nation at Risk: The Imperative for Educational Reform* (Washington: Government Printing Office, 1983), p. 5.

[4]John E. Chubb and Terry M. Moe, *Politics, Markets and America's Schools* (Washington: Brookings Institution, 1990), p. 8.

Responding to *A Nation at Risk* and other reports, state after state adopted major reforms and substantially increased funding for kindergarten through 12th grade (K–12) education. But a decade later, little has changed: American students are still "not learning enough, they are not learning the right things, and, most debilitating of all, they are not learning how to learn," say Chubb and Moe.[5] They base their depressing conclusions on an exhaustive analysis of available research, including a database covering more than 20,000 students, teachers, and principals in a nationwide sample of 500 schools.[6]

Prominent figures in business and higher education echo these concerns. Consider, for example, this bleak assessment of government education from Benno Schmidt, former president of Yale University:

> The evidence that U.S. schools are not working well is depressingly familiar. One in five young Americans drops out of high school. Nearly half of all high school graduates have not mastered seventh-grade arithmetic. American 13-year-olds place near the bottom in science and math achievement in international comparisons. One-third of 17-year-olds cannot place France on a map of the world. Only about one in 10 high school graduates can write a reasonably coherent paragraph or handle pre-college mathematics.
>
> Of even greater concern, perhaps, is that many schools have wavered from liberal educational purposes. They are hunkered down instead in a shortsighted utilitarianism that leaves little room for the free play of young people's curiosity, respect for knowledge as a good in itself, and the cultivation of the imagination and the sense of beauty.[7]

Lance Izumi tells of a conversation with a new elementary school teacher in the Grant Union School District in Sacramento. Neither she nor her students had any textbooks at all. Izumi notes, sadly, that other teachers share her predicament—even as spending on schools has skyrocketed.[8] Meanwhile, a grand jury investigation of

[5]Ibid., p. 1.

[6]Ibid., p. ix.

[7]Benno C. Schmidt, Jr., "Educational Innovation for Profit," *Wall Street Journal*, June 5, 1992, p. A12.

[8]Lance Izumi, "California's Education System: Where Does All the Money Go?" Golden State Center for Policy Studies Briefing no. 1992–11, February 19, 1992, pp. 7–16.

that district, the fourth such inquiry in 10 years, found that it has such poor internal financial controls that it cannot account for the expenditure of hundreds of thousands of dollars of its budget.[9]

Schools without books can hardly teach children to read. Even schools with books, all in all, aren't doing an adequate job of it. According to "Adult Literacy in America," a 1993 report from the National Center for Education Statistics, nearly half of adult Americans are barely literate, with such limited reading and writing skills that they cannot perform simple tasks like writing a letter explaining a billing error.[10]

It is becoming increasingly difficult to exaggerate the magnitude of the disaster in the government schools. Although some splendid exceptions do a fine job for the fortunate few, government schools as a whole are doing a mediocre job, and some of them are degenerating into holding pens or virtual war zones. As *U.S. News* notes, "The nation's faith in its public schools is fading fast. A steady stream of reports from the nation's classrooms about drugs, violence, bureaucratic bloat and ill-educated students is eroding public confidence. . . . More and more parents say they would opt for a private school if they could afford one."[11]

Parents want schools to help prepare their children for productive work, for higher education, and for responsible citizenship. We now examine government school performance in each of these areas.

Preparation for the Workforce

Employer Needs

Is the government school system preparing students for productive employment? Ask the employers. David Kearns, former chairman of Xerox:

> Public education has put this country at a terrible competitive disadvantage. The American workforce is running out of qualified people. If current demographic and economic

[9]See "What Grand Juries Think about California Education," a fact sheet issued by Yes on 174, A Better Choice, drawing on research by the Claremont Institute.

[10]Tamara Henry, "90 Million Can Barely Read, Write," *USA Today*, September 9, 1993, p. 1A; "If U Cn Reed Thiz Storie," *U.S. News & World Report*, September 20, 1993, p. 10.

[11]"The Flight from Public Schools," pp. 66–67.

trends continue, American business will have to hire a million new workers a year who can't read, write, or count. Teaching them how—and absorbing the lost productivity while they're learning—will cost industry $25 billion a year. . . . Teaching new workers basic skills is doing the schools' product-recall work for them. And frankly, I resent it.[12]

Fortune magazine:

As a major contributor of tax dollars to public education, corporate America is getting a lousy return on its investment. Not only are schools today not preparing kids for jobs, they aren't even teaching them to read and write.[13]

USA Today:

U.S. corporations spend $25 billion a year teaching employees skills they should have learned at school. Motorola spends $50 million a year teaching seventh-grade math and English to 12,500 factory workers—half its hourly employees. Kodak is teaching 2,500 how to read and write.[14]

Motorola established its massive remedial education program not as a fringe benefit but as a matter of corporate survival. To stay competitive, the company was decentralizing authority, eliminating middle management, and giving more freedom and responsibility to individual workers. But a strange thing happened on the road to increased productivity: with "many fewer supervisors," workers needed to make "intensive use of computer terminals," meaning that "everyone had to read the screens and type in text and data." Suddenly "Motorola was in real trouble." To upper management's

---

[12]David L. Kearns, "A Business Perspective on American Schooling," *Education Week* 7, no. 30 (1988): 32, 34. Kearns later served in the U.S. Department of Education during the Bush administration.

[13]Nancy J. Perry, "The Education Crisis: What Business Can Do," *Fortune*, July 4, 1988, pp. 70–81.

[14]*USA Today*, 3 February 1989, p. 1B. The statements from David Kearns, *Fortune*, and *USA Today* are quoted by Joseph Murphy, "The Educational Reform Movement of the 1980s: A Comprehensive Analysis," in *The Educational Reform Movement of the 1980s*, ed. Joseph Murphy (Berkeley, Calif.: McCutchan Publishing Corp., 1990).

astonishment, many workers simply could not read the screens, type in text, or determine what data to enter.[15]

Motorola management is not alone. A 1991 Committee for Economic Development survey found that fewer than 1 out of 4 employers consider high school graduates adept at math, and only 1 out of 10 say they write well.[16] These perceptions are confirmed by the National Assessment of Educational Progress (NAEP), a battery of standardized tests the U.S. Department of Education uses to measure skills of 9-, 13-, and 17-year-olds in math, science, and reading. "National Assessment of Educational *Progress*" is an optimistic title; for the past decade, there has been no progress to assess. Scores are flat, and *Business Week* calls student performance "stubbornly mediocre."[17] Albert Shanker, president of the American Federation of Teachers, acknowledges this. "Only 5 percent of our graduating twelfth graders can solve problems using algebra and geometry," he says, "and half of those who are about to graduate from high school cannot do what NAEP calls seventh grade work."[18]

These statistics summarize a host of individual disappointments, even tragedies. The broader implications of this wasted human potential are sobering. Ray Marshall, secretary of labor in the Carter administration, and Marc Tucker, executive director of the Carnegie Forum on Education and the Economy, argue:

> The future now belongs to societies that organize themselves for learning. What we know ... holds the key to economic progress.... More than ever before, nations that want high incomes and full employment must develop policies that emphasize the acquisition of knowledge and skills by everyone, not just a select few.... Our most formidable competitors know this. Many newly industrialized countries know it and are vaulting forward as a result. But the United States does not.[19]

International Competitiveness

In an increasingly united world economy, where goods, capital, information, and ideas flow ever more freely across national borders,

[15]Ray Marshall and Marc Tucker, *Thinking for a Living* (New York: Basic Books, 1992), p. 100.

[16]"Saving Our Schools," *Business Week*, September 14, 1992, p. 70.

[17]Ibid.

[18]Albert Shanker, *New Republic*, October 28, 1991.

[19]Marshall and Tucker, p. xiii.

highly valued work will go to highly skilled workers. A nation's wealth will depend on its brain, not its brawn—not on tangible possessions like raw materials, but on the intelligence, creativity, and productivity of its people. In the information age, with computer and communications technology converging, what is known somewhere will soon be known everywhere. The simpler a process or product, the sooner and cheaper it will be imitated. Economic advantage will go to those on the leading edge, the discoverers, the creators. Will they be Americans?

The U.S. Department of Education reported in 1993 that many large employers, including Bell Laboratories, Texas Instruments, and IBM, are being forced to fill research jobs with people educated outside the United States.[20] There are simply not enough American students with the necessary proficiency in math and science. The 1992 International Assessment of Educational Progress found that "American 13-year-olds rank among the lowest of students in 15 industrialized nations in science, finishing behind countries like South Korea and Hungary," U.S. News reports. "In mathematics, American students placed next to last."[21] During the 1992 presidential campaign Roger Altman, an economic adviser to then-governor Clinton, wrote: "The knowledge and skills of our work force are America's most crucial economic resource, but the widening achievement gap between our students and those in the rest of the industrialized world is beyond dispute."[22]

Beyond dispute, perhaps; yet for two decades the education establishment has been disputing it. In 1982 Barbara Lerner, who had been documenting the decline of student performance on domestic tests, decided to investigate how American students compared with those in other nations.

> So I dug up the data—not what the ed-biz people said about them, but the scores themselves, ours and those of all foreign students who took the same tests, and painstakingly compared them. I published the results in the *Public Interest* in fall 1982, and summed them up this way: "The results for

[20]Lynda Richardson, "Public Schools Are Failing Brightest Students, a Federal Study Says," *New York Times*, November 5, 1993.

[21]"Back to First Principles," *U.S. News & World Report*, November 8, 1993, p. 72.

[22]Roger C. Altman, "In Defense of Clintonomics, an Investment in Growth," *Wall Street Journal*, July 16, 1992, p. A11.

the U.S. were these: Out of 19 tests, we were never ranked first or second; we came in dead last three times, and, if comparisons are limited to other developed nations only, the U.S. ranked at the bottom seven times."

That's the sentence the Excellence Commission quoted in *A Nation at Risk,* the one that made headlines, shook America awake, and made everyone see the threat our poor academic performance poses to our economy, our standard of living, and our place in the world.

A Nation at Risk came out in spring 1983. It accepted my conclusion as fact, and opposition melted away so quickly that most people don't remember there was a debate about whether I was right or not, but there was, and it was a hot one. Brief, but hot. In 1982, no one knew how badly our kids were faring, and a significant portion of the education establishment was determined to keep it that way.[23]

Our international standing wouldn't be so troubling if we were improving or at least holding steady. But we're getting worse! The International Association for the Evaluation of Educational Achievement (IEA) performed detailed studies comparing achievement of 14-year-old students from various nations in the sciences. From 1970 to 1984, 8 of the 10 countries examined registered significant gains, some of them substantial. The results for one country remained flat. "For the United States," the IEA noted, "there is evidence of a sizeable drop in level of achievement." While other students showed an average gain equivalent to approximately half a year of schooling in science, American students lost the equivalent of two years.[24]

During the drive to qualify the Parental Choice in Education Initiative for the California ballot, I occasionally raised this issue on the debate trail. Opponents in the education establishment insisted that I was comparing apples and oranges. Some debate opponents even claimed that the declining scores represented good news. Their line of argument goes like this: Other nations test only their college-bound students, and that's after admitting only their brightest into the college prep track; their other students are shunted into dead-end vocational or technical programs. America, in contrast, gives

[23]Barbara Lerner, "The 'Opportunity' Fantasy," *National Review,* July 19, 1993, p. 42.

[24]J. P. Keeves, *Learning Science in a Changing World: Cross-National Studies of Science Achievement, 1970 to 1984* (n.p.: International Association for the Evaluation of Educational Achievement, n.d.), p. 14 and Figure 3.2.

everyone a chance; anyone can go to college, and almost everyone takes the tests. If you compare *top* American students to their foreign counterparts, my debate opponents always said, we look fine.

Even if that were true, it would not explain away our declining performance; but it is not true. "America's *top* high school science students ranked below those of nearly all other countries in a new comparison of scores from an international test released here last week," reported *Education Week* in 1988. Sixteen countries were tested. American students ranked 13th in physics, 14th in chemistry, and dead last in biology. "The achievement levels are particularly 'discouraging,' the study's authors note, since the American students in the comparison were drawn from the small proportion of the nation's high-school students enrolled in advanced science courses."[25] A 1993 U.S. Department of Education study reports similar findings. Among top students from 13 countries, the Americans ranked 9th in physics, 11th in chemistry, and 13th in biology. Again, these were high school seniors taking advanced placement courses.[26] In short, America's best science students are the industrialized world's worst.

Math scores tell the same story. In elementary school: Researchers at the University of Michigan and the University of California, Irvine, studied math achievement among elementary school students in the United States, Japan, and China in 1980 and again in 1990. During that decade of supposed education reform, there was "virtually no improvement in math achievement among American students," who remain outperformed by the Japanese and Chinese.[27] In junior high: "At a time when economic growth is increasingly dependent on mastery of science and technology, U.S. eighth graders' knowledge and understanding of mathematics is below that of most of their counterparts in other industrialized countries (12 out of 14)."[28] In

[25]*Education Week,* March 19, 1988, p. 4, reporting on a 1986 survey. Cited by Murphy, p. 11.

[26]Tamara Henry, "Gifted Kids Are Bored by U.S. Schools," *USA Today,* November 5, 1993, p. 1A.

[27]United Press International dispatch in the *Deseret News* (Salt Lake City, Utah), January 1, 1993, p. A12, reporting on a study by Professors Harold W. Stevenson and Shin-Ying Lee of Michigan and Chuansheng Chen of the University of California, Irvine.

[28]Carnegie Forum on Education and the Economy (1986, p. 16), cited by Murphy, p. 12.

high school calculus and algebra: "Contrary to widespread opinion, it isn't clear that our top students compare well with the top students of other nations." One study shows American seniors ninth out of nine on international calculus and algebra tests.[29] Another shows them 12th out of 13 in geometry and calculus, 13th out of 13 in algebra.[30]

In the most recent international comparison by the Organization for Economic Cooperation and Development (OECD), American students did rather well in reading and near average in science. Unfortunately, this apparent improvement occurred only because the OECD omitted five countries that had outperformed the United States in previous surveys, including Hungary, Korea, and Taiwan.[31]

In summary, national borders are becoming less and less relevant to the world economy; today's students will be competing in an international marketplace tomorrow. They are poorly prepared for it. Studies ranking the educational achievement of students from various countries put the Americans near or at the bottom. Apologists for the government school system quibble about the methodology of the studies and the relative rankings of the various countries— but they never seriously argue that the Americans rank first.

Preparation for Higher Education

Current Perfomance

The government school system does a poor job of preparing students for the workforce. It does a poor job of preparing them for a marketplace that includes strong and improving international competitors. It also does a poor job of preparing them for college. On this issue I speak from personal experience.

I love teaching. Before going to law school I had intended to get a Ph.D. in English, and for a while I taught English 115, the standard reading and writing course at Brigham Young University. BYU is the nation's largest private university, with about 27,000 students, and it is fairly competitive academically. I still remember the enthusiasm with which I prepared for my first class of incoming freshmen. Remembering my own English classes with Mr. Godwin and Ms.

---

[29]Ibid., p. 13; citations to several studies omitted.
[30]Henry, "Gifted Kids Are Bored by U.S. Schools," p. 1A.
[31]"False Positive," *Washington Post*, January 23, 1994.

Butcher at Oakmont High, I expected my new students to have no problem writing half a dozen essays and a research paper. I consulted with several professors to make sure that the class syllabus I had prepared was realistic.

Class began. My students were utterly unacquainted with good literature, but they were bright and willing to read. Things were fine until they turned in their first essays. I still remember the profound woe with which I realized that the first few papers were not aberrations. Correcting them was simply impossible; there wasn't that much time in the semester. Even commenting on them . . . I hardly knew where to begin. Perhaps they just didn't take the first assignment seriously?

The next papers dispelled that notion. Half my students were having trouble putting coherent thoughts into coherent sentences, let alone paragraphs and essays. Out went the syllabus; in came a new emphasis on the fundamentals. Apparently I would be teaching high school writing, not college writing.

They made substantial progress. Several of them told me that I had much to do with that, which was gratifying. But I felt badly that they missed the class promised on the first syllabus. We never read most of the mind-expanding literature I had originally scheduled, never did the kind of writing I had anticipated. They had been cheated. All of them were bright and willing to work, and most of them were capable of writing well; they proved it, after intensive remedial work, later in the semester. Why was I teaching them what they should have learned in high school? What was the government school system doing with them all that time?

Shortly after announcing his resignation as president of Yale University, Benno Schmidt lamented that "high school students today are posting lower SAT scores than a generation ago," and their lower scores clearly reflect poorer preparation for college.[32] The SAT (Scholastic Aptitude Test) is the best-known measure of American high school students intending to proceed to college. From 1960 to 1992, the average math score on the SAT dropped 22 points (from 498 to 476), and the average verbal score plummeted 54 points (from 477 to 423), for a precipitous combined drop of 76 points (975 to 899). Moreover, the grading procedure changed during that time;

---

[32]Schmidt, p. A12.

had it remained constant, the current numbers would be even lower, by an estimated 18 to 30 points.[33] (See figure 2.1)

When I raised this issue in debates on the Parental Choice in Education Initiative, my counterparts in the education establishment replied that since so many more minority and disadvantaged students were taking the test, a decline in average scores was inevitable. In support of this contention many of them cited *Perspectives on Education in America,* a study conducted by Sandia National Laboratories. Peter Huber summarizes their argument: "Average scores

Figure 2.1
SCHOLASTIC APTITUDE TEST SCORES 1960–92

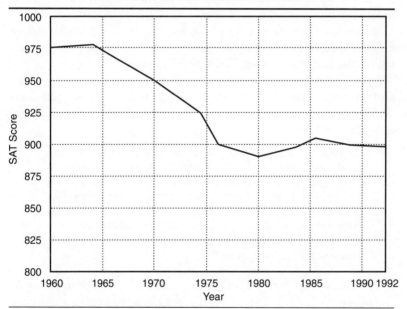

SOURCE: Educational Testing Service.

NOTE: SAT scores for 1961–67 are averages for all students; subsequent scores are averages for college-bound seniors.

[33]Source for scores: The College Board. See William J. Bennett, "The Index of Leading Cultural Indicators," Empower America, Heritage Foundation, and Free Congress Foundation, Washington, March 1993, p. 17, citing Charles Murray, "What's Really behind the SAT-Score Decline?" *Public Interest,* no. 106 (Winter 1992). In California, average verbal scores declined from 464 in 1972 to 424 in 1988; average math scores declined from 493 in 1972 to 484 in 1988. James S. Fay, ed., *California Almanac,* 5th ed. (Santa Barbara: Pacific Data Resources, 1991), p. 68.

have been declining, but your 'average' student is doing better, or at least as well as he ever did. What has changed is not student performance but demographics. Minority students, whose scores are rising faster, but from a lower base, are showing up in test rooms in higher numbers than they used to."[34]

The graph accompanying Huber's article does indeed show modest improvement in average SAT scores for most minority subpopulations—but it also shows a clear decline in average scores for whites.[35] Moreover, as Daniel J. Singal asks, "Can we really explain the sharp decline in college-entrance-exam scores by pointing to the inner cities, where only a tiny fraction of students even take the Scholastic Aptitude Test?"[36] No, answers Thomas Sowell: "Unfortunately for this argument, test scores have been declining *at the top*. Twenty years ago, more than 116,000 students scored above 600 on the SAT (out of a possible 800). Today, with slightly more students taking the test, fewer than 75,000 score that high."[37]

Average SAT scores peaked in 1963, declined through the sixties and seventies, stabilized in the mid-eighties, and resumed their decline in the nineties. Students at the top led the decline.[38] Singal elaborates:

> In 1972, of the high school seniors taking the SAT 11.4 percent had verbal scores over 600; by 1983 the number had dropped to 6.9 percent, and, despite modest gains in the mid-1980s, it remains in that disheartening vicinity. That's a decline of nearly 40 percent. The decline since the mid-1960s has probably been closer to 50 percent, but unfortunately the College Board changed its reporting system in 1972, and earlier data isn't available.[39]

In other words, today's brightest students are not performing as well as yesterday's. Taking the egalitarian ideal to a curious extreme, the education establishment justifies the decline by saying, in essence, that the best students may have gotten worse, but at least

[34]Peter Huber, "The Lie of Averages," *Forbes*, December 20, 1993, p. 252.
[35]Ibid.
[36]Daniel J. Singal, "The Other Crisis in American Education," *Atlantic Monthly*, November 1991, pp. 59–60.
[37]Thomas Sowell, "Excuses, Excuses," *Forbes*, October 14, 1991, p. 43.
[38]Ibid.
[39]Singal, p. 61.

the worst students are included. Now, I wholeheartedly endorse making educational opportunity broadly available; that is, after all, a fundamental purpose of school choice. But SAT scores could and should be much higher at both ends of the scale. Failing to challenge top students does nothing to help low achievers. How do we attain excellence if we restrain those capable of excelling?

"Gifted Kids Are Bored by U.S. Schools."[40] "U.S. Is Failing to Challenge Its Smartest Kids."[41] These headlines summarize the findings of "National Excellence: A Case for Developing America's Talent," the U.S. Department of Education's 1993 report on the status of gifted and talented students stuck in the government schools. Gifted elementary school students are required to do time in the classroom even though they have mastered 35 percent to 50 percent of the curriculum before the school year starts. The report recommends that gifted students be identified and given a more challenging curriculum.

Will it happen? "I like sure bets," says B. Meredith Burke, an adjunct faculty member at San Jose State University. "One is that [this study] will be ignored. No, make that rejected." Why?

> For at least half a century, we as a nation have continually rejected research findings about the gifted because reality refuses to be politically correct. Americans persist in applying the political concept "all men are created equal" to the intellectual realm, with painful and costly results. Even more perversely, we loosen this straitjacket for those who fall below the mean while tightening it for those who land above.
>
> For five decades educators have discounted the findings of the definitive continuing study of gifted children, begun in the 1920s. They have actually abandoned grade acceleration, a practice strongly endorsed by study director Lewis Terman. They assail "ability grouping" while encouraging the proliferation of "special programs" for the learning disabled, for those of limited English proficiency, and for those otherwise handicapped. . . .
>
> Most programs for gifted students . . . have been inadequate. Although now offered by about two-thirds of public schools, they are generally nominal—two to three hours a week—and unrelated to the scholastic demands of children

[40]Henry, "Gifted Kids Are Bored by U.S. Schools," p. 1A.
[41]Richardson.

21

> who have mastered at least half the curriculum before the
> start of a school year.[42]

When the most promising students are treated as fungible commodities, is it any wonder that they grow bored and tune out? There are two crises in American education, Daniel J. Singal argues. Almost everyone is aware of the highly visible one: that of the disadvantaged, mostly minority children attending dysfunctional, dead-end inner-city schools. The second crisis, in contrast, is almost "invisible," involving college-bound students from supposedly good schools. They now enter college so poorly prepared that they perform "far below potential, often to the point of functional disability," Singal says. "We tend to assume that with their high aptitude for learning, they should be able to fend for themselves. However, the experience of the past fifteen years has proved decisively that they can't."[43]

While teaching my freshman English course, I wondered whether I was too demanding. Were my expectations unrealistic? Was my experience exceptional? Singal says that I was not alone:

> Does a loss of sixty points on the verbal SAT translate into
> a significant difference in a student's educational experience
> at college? The testimony of those who teach at the college
> level suggests that the answer is yes.
>
> Those who tend to dismiss those sixty lost SAT points as
> insignificant haven't seen a college term paper lately. It's not
> that freshmen in 1991 are unable to read or write. . . . But is
> that enough for college? Do they have sufficient command
> of the English language to comprehend a college-level text,
> think through a complex issue, or express a reasonably
> sophisticated argument on paper? Those of us who were
> teaching in the early 1970s can attest that the overwhelming
> majority of freshmen at the more selective colleges arrived
> with such "advanced" skills. Now only a handful come so
> equipped.[44]

Singal laments the "impoverishment of language" and "downturn in reasoning skills" among entering college students. Think of the

---

[42]B. Meredith Burke, "Gifted Kids, the Hidden Disadvantaged," *Wall Street Journal*, December 8, 1993, p. A14.

[43]Singal, p. 59.

[44]Ibid., p. 61.

wasted potential and lost opportunities. "These complaints," he says, "are amply substantiated by data from the National Assessment of Educational Progress. On one test of analytic writing measuring 'the ability to provide evidence, reason logically, and make a well-developed point,' only *four tenths of one percent* of eleventh graders performed at the 'elaborated' (what I believe should be considered college-freshman) level."[45]

Historical Performance

Today's best students are not performing as well as yesterday's. Empirical evidence is available but probably superfluous. "Pick up a fifth-grade math or rhetoric textbook from 1850," says John Taylor Gatto, New York State's teacher of the year, "and you'll see that the texts were pitched then on what would today be considered college level."[46] Or just ask parents whether their school-age children today are receiving the quality of education they did a generation ago. Many will say no, and they will be right. One such parent is Barbara Bronson Gray, who tells us about her son's government school:

> It's sitting on my desk, this colorful cardboard crown that looks like the kind of craft a child would make in a summer park program.
> But it represents two hours of public school effort by a third-grade student, my son. It shows why California schools are failing our students. . . .
> This sort of activity isn't an anomaly. . . . This is in a school district that offers the children fewer than 170 full days of school a year.
> Remember book reports? You not only had to remember what you read, but learn to summarize and analyze and get it down on paper. Not any more. At this school, the kids make mobiles and dioramas to illustrate the book's concept.
> As for writing, most of what is taught is creative writing, journal writing, free expression. Learn the structure of a paragraph? How to research a topic? How to argue a point? No, that's old-fashioned. Boring. We'll teach that—someday, in context—the educators say.[47]

[45]Ibid., p. 62; emphasis in the original.

[46]John Taylor Gatto, *Dumbing Us Down* (Philadelphia: New Society Publishers, 1992), p. 13.

[47]Barbara Bronson Gray, "And They Call This a Model School," *Wall Street Journal,* July 22, 1992, p. A10.

Ms. Bronson Gray informs us that this was considered a model school! It won awards and plaudits from the education professionals, but not from her. Her two children, she says, will be transferring to an independent school.

I heard stories like hers time and again throughout the California campaign. One radio talk show caller, frustrated with his local government school, exclaimed, "I'm not talking about turning my kids into geniuses, I just want them to read!"[48]

American education wasn't always this way. Author Avis Carlson describes the grand achievement of earning her eighth-grade diploma in a small Kansas town in 1907. She had to define "panegyric," "talisman," "triton," and "misconception"; calculate the interest on an 8 percent note for $900 running 2 years, 2 months, and 6 days; name countries producing large quantities of wheat, cotton, coal, and tea; "give a brief account of the colleges, printing, and religion in the colonies prior to the American Revolution"; and "name the principal political questions which have been advocated since the Civil War and the party which advocated each." David Boaz asks, "Can we imagine applicants to Harvard passing that test today?"[49]

Empirical evidence supports these anecdotal accounts of diminishing challenge and declining performance over the years. Cornell University sociologist Donald Hayes took 766 elementary and secondary school texts published from 1860 to 1991, then designed a computerized scoring system to determine the comparative difficulty of reading them. "The texts for the fourth through eighth grades have been declining since 1965," he reports, "and now are the simplest they've ever been." Today's sixth graders are using texts equivalent in difficulty to those used by fourth graders in 1896. "It's not that students are any dumber than they used to be," Prof. Hayes says, "but that they haven't gotten from the schools the depth of knowledge they used to get."[50]

---

[48]The caller was David from Bloomington; I was a guest on "Inland Empire Talk," radio station 1240 AM, in the San Bernardino area, on February 20, 1992.

[49]Avis Carlson, *Small World Long Gone: A Family Record of an Era* (Evanston, Ill.: Scori Press, 1975), pp. 83–84; quoted in David Boaz, "The Public School Monopoly: America's Berlin Wall," in *Liberating Schools: Education in the Inner City*, ed. David Boaz (Washington: Cato Institute, 1991), p. 3.

[50]Jerry E. Bishop, "Low SAT Verbal Scores? Blame Simple Textbooks," *Wall Street Journal*, November 29, 1993, p. B1.

Not surprisingly, as textbook difficulty has diminished, so has student achievement. Students learned more a generation ago than they do today. The disparity is reflected in declining scores on the Stanford Achievement Test (not to be confused with the Scholastic Aptitude Test, or SAT, which is a college entrance exam). Singal writes:

> From the 1920s to the late 1960s American children taking the Stanford made significant gains in their test performance. They made so much progress, in fact, that as the test was revised each decade, the level of difficulty of the questions was increased substantially, reflecting the increasing level of challenge of the instructional materials being used in the schools.
>
> From the late 1960s to the early 1980s, however, we managed to squander the better part of that progress, with the greatest losses coming in the high schools. . . . The test numbers substantiate what the National Commission on Excellence in Education concluded—quoting the education analyst Paul Copperman—in 1983 in *A Nation at Risk*: "Each generation of Americans has outstripped its parents in education, in literacy, and in economic attainment. For the first time in the history of our country, the educational skills of one generation will not surpass, will not equal, will not even approach, those of their parents."[51]

Preparation for Responsible Citizenship

The preservation of freedom in a constitutional republic requires an educated electorate. Ignorance and liberty cannot coexist for long. Thus, ever since the American states won their independence, leading citizens have identified preparation for responsible citizenship as a key purpose—perhaps *the* key purpose—of schooling. As historian Page Smith writes in *The Shaping of America*:

> Those Founding Fathers who discussed education (and most of them did) were agreed on one basic tenet: a republican form of government could not survive without an educated citizenry. The primary purpose of an education was to enable a citizen to properly discharge his responsibilities as a member of a free society.[52]

[51]Singal, p. 60.

[52]Page Smith, *The Shaping of America: A People's History of the Young Republic*, (New York: McGraw Hill, 1980), vol. 3, p. 353.

The founders considered the powers of government safe only so long as ultimate sovereignty resided among properly educated citizens. Smith summarizes Thomas Jefferson's expression of this view:

> In every government there was "some germ of corruption and degeneracy." All governments degenerated when entrusted to the "rulers of the people alone." People as citizens must be properly informed of the workings of their governments and actively involved on every level. They were the "only safe depositories" of the powers of government. "And to render them safe their minds must be improved to a certain degree."[53]

So important was this improvement that Noah Webster argued that "such a system of education as gives every citizen an opportunity of acquiring knowledge and fitting himself for places of trust" was a "*sine qua non* of the existence of the American republics."[54]

To the founders, preparation for responsible citizenship required not only academic training but cultivation of the civic virtues. To this end some, like Benjamin Rush, favored schooling incorporating religious instruction; others, like Thomas Jefferson, preferred a secular course of study. Despite their differences on the role of religion in schooling, virtually all the founders who expressed views on education wanted schools to teach fundamental values and provide moral instruction. Benjamin Franklin, for example, expected the ideal course of study "to fix in the minds of youth deep impressions of the beauty and usefulness of virtue of all kinds, public spirit, fortitude, etc." Along with academic instruction, Franklin urged that there "should be constantly inculcated and cultivated that benignity of mind which shows itself in searching for and seizing every opportunity to serve and oblige."[55]

In his "Circular to the States," issued upon completion of the Revolutionary War, General Washington identified four prerequisites to the continued independence of the United States. Among these was "the prevalence of that pacific and friendly disposition among the people of the United States which will induce them to

[53]Ibid., p. 358.
[54]Ibid., p. 356.
[55]Ibid., p. 355.

forget their local prejudices and policies, to make those mutual concessions which are requisite to the general prosperity, and in some instances, to sacrifice their individual advantages to the interest of the community."[56]

The civic virtues advocated by Washington and Franklin seem in short supply today, but surely they are no less needed now than then. Parents appropriately expect schools, in the process of helping to prepare their children for productive work or higher education, or both, to foster such virtues. Schools can and should reinforce the common values necessary to the perpetuation of a free republic. Among these are an understanding of the rule of law; an appreciation of liberty and the constitutional principles that preserve it; and respect for the life, liberty, property, and opinions of others.

Do the government schools cultivate these qualities in their students? Not really. A dumbing down of values and expectations has paralleled the dumbing down of the curriculum. The predominant trend in government schools is to maintain a posture of undiscriminating neutrality on any matter remotely moral; these things are said to be matters of opinion, personal, relative. Intellectual inquiry and reasoned debate are out; exploration of feelings is in. School personnel can safely promote such politically correct causes as environmentalism or such politically correct values as tolerance of the unusual, and they can usually require appropriate behavior in the classroom; but the cultivation of any qualities of character beyond these is considered oppressive, improper, and quaint.

Even so, defenders of today's government schools argue that they at least promote such values as mutual respect and appreciation of diversity. Curiously, however, many of those most loudly proclaiming the benefits of the common school experience prevent their own children from enjoying it. During the campaign against California's Proposition 174, the *Wall Street Journal* notes:

> Anti-174 pitchmen rhapsodize about the value of the "common school" experience, in which shared values are nurtured in a diverse student body. In reality, the content-free education now mandated by many districts makes it easier to smuggle a gun into a classroom than to allow a teacher to discuss moral values.

[56]George Washington, "Circular to the States," June 8, 1783; cited in *The Spirit of 'Seventy-Six*, ed. Henry Steele Commager and Richard B. Morris (New York: Harper & Row, 1975), p. 1285.

> Phil Angelides, former chairman of the California Democratic Party, is one who warns voters not to abandon "the tradition of the common school." He says, "I am committed to giving the public schools more time to reform themselves." However, he sheepishly admits his own children attend private schools, mumbling "there are a lot of problems in the Sacramento system."
>
> John Mockler, a Sacramento-based lobbyist for the Los Angeles Unified School District, is also concerned with the quality of local schools. He worries that vouchers will mean "the nature of the common experience is gone," but his daughter attends a private school.[57]

The *Journal* notes that those most intimately involved with the operation of government schools are the most likely to send their own children elsewhere.

> The California State Census Data Center, after analyzing the 1990 Census, found that about 18.2% of the state's public school teachers send their children to private schools. That's nearly twice the statewide average for all households, which is 9.7%.[58]

Academic opportunity is probably the primary reason for this, but no doubt other factors play a part. The common school experience is not always what its defenders claim. Perhaps the most troubling evidence of something gone awry is the dramatically diminishing respect for life and property evidenced on school grounds.

My friend Matt Harris once mused that he should write a pamphlet called, "Reading, Writing, and Dodging Bullets: A Survival Guide to the Public Schools." He wasn't joking. During the 1987–88 school year, 64,783 violent crimes, occurred in California government schools. In addition to the violent crimes, there were 74,894 property crimes. Adding other crimes gives a total of 162,061 criminal incidents. To put that in perspective, California has 7,125 government schools. That means an average of 23 reported crimes per school per year.[59] Of course, some students aren't fortunate enough to attend average schools. And those figures are a few years old. Nobody thinks things have improved since then.

[57]"Teacher Knows Best," editorial, *Wall Street Journal*, October 25, 1993, p. A14.
[58]Ibid., p. A14.
[59]Fay, pp. 64–74.

As of 1993, the nation's 85,000 government schools were experiencing more than 3 million crimes annually, or more than 35 crimes each.[60] "Behind the rash of violence," says one news account,

> is a startling shift in adolescent attitudes. Suddenly—chillingly—respect for life has ebbed sharply among teenagers—and not just in embattled inner cities. Twenty percent of the suburban high schoolers surveyed by Tulane researchers Joseph Sheley and M. Dwayne Smith endorsed shooting someone "who has stolen something from you." Eight percent believed that it is all right to shoot a person "who had done something to offend or insult you." Concluded the researchers: "One is struck less by the armament [among today's teenagers] than by the evident willingness to pull the trigger."[61]

A Gallup poll asked parents of elementary students which problems facing the schools concerned them most. Nearly 70 percent named violence.[62] Notwithstanding parental concern, student fear, and public outrage, the consequences of juvenile violent crime remain serious only for the victims, not the perpetrators. Youths accused of violent crime are twice as likely to be put on probation or set free as to remain in custody. Only 3 percent are tried in adult courts.[63]

How do students learn respect for the life, liberty, and property of others in such an environment? They don't. William K. Kilpatrick, a professor of education at Boston College, writes of the high school students who cried at their 15-year-old classmate's arraignment—not because of the murder he had committed, but because his bail was high. An isolated incident? Kilpatrick reports that "a recent, national study of 1,700 sixth- to ninth-graders revealed that a majority of boys considered rape to be acceptable under certain conditions. Astoundingly, many of the girls agreed." What is going on? It is no mystery, Kilpatrick states:

[60]Thomas Toch, "Violence in Schools," *U.S. News & World Report*, November 8, 1993, p. 31.

[61]Ibid., p. 32.

[62]"Drugs Top Worries about Elementary School," *Wall Street Journal*, September 27, 1993, p. B1.

[63]Toch, p. 37.

Many of today's young people have a difficult time seeing any moral dimension to their actions. There are a number of reasons why that's true, but none more prominent than a failed system of education that eschews teaching children the traditional moral values that bind Americans together as a society and a culture. That failed approach, called "decision-making," was introduced in schools 25 years ago. It tells children to decide for themselves what is right and what is wrong. It replaced "character education." Character education didn't ask children to reinvent the moral wheel. . . .

Teaching right from wrong has as much bearing on a culture's survival as teaching reading, writing or science, and there exists a great wealth of knowledge about how to do it.[64]

But the government school system refuses to do so, abetting the disappearance of civility and creating a moral vacuum into which violence and cruelty have rushed. One Los Angeles father, Bennie Murray, told me that his daughter, though eager to learn, had grown so afraid of her government junior high school that she refused to attend. Fortunately he was able to transfer her to an independent school. Although she seemed to be learning more in the new school, academics played no role in the transfer. "Forget education," Bennie told me. "We just wanted her to be safe."[65]

Obviously the government schools are victims, to some extent, of exogenous factors. The dramatic rise of illegitimate births and the dramatic decline of social order have consequences that do not stop at the schoolhouse door. The family, not the school, bears primary and ultimate responsibility for shaping the character of the child. But why is it that children who do not feel safe in urban government schools can transfer to independent schools and thrive?

One reason is that independent schools tend to have a clear sense of mission and concomitantly high expectations. Directly, through discipline, and indirectly, through the very quality of the learning environment, they tend to instill respect for self, for others, for order, and for law. No government school consciously or intentionally invites misbehavior, but might not the rise of moral relativism, the

[64]William K. Kilpatrick, "Turning Out Moral Illiterates," *Los Angeles Times*, July 20, 1993, p. B7.

[65]Bennie and Chawna Murray recounted their experience in a CNN interview on January 23, 1992.

30

decline of discipline, and the virtual disappearance of character education in the schools play a part in poor citizenship?

To the extent that government schools do involve themselves with values, all too often they undercut, rather than reinforce, what some parents are trying to teach at home. This is especially evident in sex education programs which treat human intimacy as a mechanical matter, ignoring a possible moral component. Many parents deeply resent government school overreaching in this area. While I lived in the Los Angeles Unified School District boundaries, the district was concerned about safe sex—so concerned, in fact, that condom distribution mattered more than keeping an eye on the massive budget. On January 27, 1992, officials of LAUSD announced an unexpected budget shortfall of $150 million. I can't decide if this newspaper account is comic or tragic:

> The Los Angeles Board of Education has appointed the accounting firm of Ernst & Young to determine, along with district staff, how large the shortfall will be, why it is occurring and how it could have been averted.
>
> The potential deficit was discovered during preparation of a mid-year review of the district's income and expenses.
>
> "We are shocked," said board member Mark Slavkin. "I will insist that there be accountability for a gap of this magnitude."[66]

Less than a week before, the same Mr. Slavkin had joined the majority of the board in approving, over the vehement objections of many district parents, the distribution of condoms on high school campuses. At the board meeting, these parents

> questioned how a district that has had to cancel courses and cut salaries because of a budget crisis could consider buying and giving away condoms. It is not known how much the condom distribution program will cost.
>
> "We're always told there's not enough money . . . where's the money coming from to pay for these condoms?" said Roosevelt High School graduate Ronnie Macias. "Students already know about condoms. We don't need them in the schools. We need books."[67]

[66]Charisse Jones, "L.A. Schools Face a New Budget Crisis," *Los Angeles Times,* January 28, 1992, p. A1.

[67]Charisse Jones, "Distribution of Condoms OKd in L.A. Schools," *Los Angeles Times,* January 22, 1992, pp. A1, A12.

31

Books. How quaint. Might their absence have anything to do with abysmal academic performance? John Taylor Gatto notices that "schools and schooling are increasingly irrelevant to the great enterprises of the planet. No one believes anymore that scientists are trained in science classes or politicians in civics classes or poets in English classes."[68] But at least they know how to apply condoms.

The Irritated Bureaucrat

Go to a school board meeting. Listen to what they talk about. From coast to coast, in large government school districts the agenda is much the same.

> During its 3½-hour October meeting, this is what the D.C. school board did: Accused a D.C. Council member of trying to usurp its fiscal power. Complained that the schools get bad press and considered how to "sell" them better. Debated whether one board member should testify before the D.C. Council, even though he had testified three weeks earlier.
> This is what the board did not talk much about: education. Children.[69]

The Los Angeles Board of Education argues over condom distribution, reapportionment, and budget deficits, but you won't hear much about teaching students to read, write, or think. Not surprisingly, parents are trying to get their kids out. A record number are obtaining permits to transfer their children into other districts. No one knows how many permits have been denied or how many parents have given up in frustration. The *Los Angeles Times* reports:

> Parents and officials in other districts complain that the Los Angeles district makes the process unnecessarily difficult. Applications must be picked up from the home school, filled out and sent to the district office. Parents must usually supply the district they are applying to with a lease or rental agreement or mortgage *and* a utility bill, a letter from their employer or child care provider.
> "There are Catch-22s all over the place," said a West Los Angeles mother who has gone through the process every year since her child, now 10, entered kindergarten. "It can take months of paperwork."

[68]Gatto, pp. 24–25.

[69]Sari Horwitz, "Some Say Board Not Taking Care of Business," *Washington Post*, November 10, 1993, p. D1.

> "I get mildly irritated when I hear complaints like that,"
> said Bice [David Bice, coordinating counselor for LAUSD's
> permits and transfers office], insisting that the district doesn't
> *try* to make it difficult.[70]

It is a classic example of bureaucratic insularity and arrogance. A mother repeatedly goes to great lengths to comply with the district's rules in negotiating its byzantine transfer process just so she can get her child into a decent school. Understandably she finds the experience frustrating. The bureaucrat is "irritated." Parents are getting irritated, too, which is why nearly one million Californians signed petitions to put the Parental Choice in Education Initiative on the ballot.

Schools should prepare students for productive work, for higher education, and for responsible citizenship. Judged by these criteria, the government school system is performing poorly.

One can hardly imagine a government school today accepting Benjamin Franklin's challenge "to fix in the minds of youth deep impressions of the beauty and usefulness of virtue of all kinds, public spirit, fortitude," or "that benignity of mind which shows itself in searching for and seizing every opportunity to serve and oblige." The blessings and responsibilities of citizens in a free society and the qualities of character necessary to its continuance receive little attention, if any; and if respect for the life, liberty, property, and opinions of others is being taught, the message seems to be missing an alarming proportion of students. Whatever the causes, the government school system is not preparing students for responsible citizenship any better than it is preparing them for work or college.

[70]Lois Timnick, "Changing Schools—Any Way They Can," *Los Angeles Times*, August 23, 1992, pp. J1, J10; emphasis in original.

33

3. Where Does All the Money Go?

With such overwhelming evidence of poor performance in the government schools, I expected the debate over the Parental Choice in Education Initiative to focus on how, not whether, to reform the system. To my surprise it took a real struggle to get that far; most "educrats"[1] would not acknowledge that performance was poor in the first place! They insisted that the schools were doing just fine. Very few parents, employers, or professors agreed, but what did they know?

I emphasize the government school system's poor performance for one reason: you cannot solve a problem if you refuse to acknowledge its existence. Obviously, the system includes dedicated teachers and principals who are trying mightily to teach their students and make their schools work. Despite their heroic efforts, however, the system is failing to educate most children adequately. In fact, the system does more to prevent quality education than to promote it.

Confronted with evidence of the government school system's poor performance, the educrats have a ready—indeed reflexive—response: they demand more money. Of course we're not doing better, they protest, when funds are so tight. Other states and other nations spend more money on schools; if we got that kind of money, we could give that kind of performance. The schools aren't failing society; society is failing the schools by not giving us the funding we need. "The underfunded public schools" is the educrats' mantra, and they seem to believe it.

[1]Short for education bureaucrat. (I do not know who coined the term; I first heard it used in a speech by Wisconsin state representative Polly Williams.) I use the word in a descriptive, not pejorative, sense. In most of my debates during the California campaign I faced representatives of the education establishment who had nothing to do with teaching children; they were highly paid administrators, consultants, or functionaries from such entities as the California School Boards Association and the Association of California School Administrators. Thus the term "educator," meaning one who educates, does not accurately describe them.

They also argue that particular reforms—higher teacher pay, stricter curriculum guidelines, competency testing, site-based management, you name it—can solve particular problems. Let's fix the present system, they say, rather than offer alternatives to it; let's not be hasty. They cite individual success stories or modest improvement on certain tests and say that things are already improving, that they just need more time. And money.

Since the educrats have a tough time admitting that anything is wrong, they have a tough time proposing how to make it right. They do have an alternative to school choice, though; they want to tinker slightly with the present system, then ask the taxpayers for a little more time and a lot more money. It doesn't sound promising, and it's not; we've already traveled that road.

American citizens have responded to the government school system's poor performance with remarkable patience and generosity. Through their elected representatives, they have implemented a host of reforms. Through their taxes, they have dramatically increased funding for the government schools. The taxpayers are getting a poor return on their investment. After a decade of reform, there is little progress to report.

The Education Reforms of the 1980s

Throughout the 1980s, hundreds of official commissions studied the government school system. Their findings, on the whole, were "scathingly critical."[2] In April 1983 the most prominent such commission, the National Commission on Excellence in Education, issued its damning report, *A Nation at Risk*. Citizens and elected officials responded, not by criticizing the government schools but by trying to help them. John Chubb and Terry Moe give this overview:

> An emerging awareness of national crisis hit with full force in the early 1980s, when widespread dissatisfaction with the state of American education was granted scientific legitimacy and political weight by a sudden flood of new studies and commission reports, all of them highly critical of the schools and arguing the urgent need for change.

[2]John E. Chubb and Terry M. Moe, *Politics, Markets and America's Schools* (Washington: Brookings Institution, 1990), pp. 9–10.

What followed has been called the "greatest and most concentrated surge of educational reform in the nation's history." State after state imposed tougher academic requirements, introduced new tests for student achievement, and increased pay and certification requirements for teachers, among other things. Some states and school districts boldly pursued more innovative solutions, from career ladders and merit pay to school-based management and magnet schools. From the vantage point of those in the educational community . . . the problem of declining academic performance had been met head-on.[3]

Joseph Murphy finds the "scope" and "momentum" of the 1980s' reform movement "unparalleled" in American history:

The attack on a host of identified problems and deficiencies has been more comprehensive, directed more at the general student population (and less at targeted groups), of greater concentrated intensity, and has spawned more activity than at any time in the past. The reform agenda also has been sustained longer than previous efforts, actually shifting into a second generation or wave of change. . . . There is greater public attention and a wider coalition of reform actors than often has been the case in the past.[4]

In California, as in many states, seemingly significant reforms were proposed, enacted, funded, and implemented. The Republican governor, the Democratic legislature, and the state's business and education leaders all supported a major reform package, which passed.[5] The reform legislation mandated a longer school day and year; imposed stricter curriculum standards, with a greater emphasis on English, math, social studies, and science; gave teachers more

---

[3]Ibid., pp. 1–2.

[4]Joseph Murphy, "The Educational Reform Movement of the 1980s: A Comprehensive Analysis," in *The Educational Reform Movement of the 1980s*, ed. Joseph Murphy (Berkeley, Calif.: McCutchan Publishing Corp., 1990), pp. 5–6.

[5]Specifically, Governor George Deukmejian and the California Business Roundtable joined in supporting S.B. 813, sponsored by State Senator Gary Hart (D-Santa Barbara), chair of the Senate Education Committee, and A.B. 70, sponsored by assembly-member Teresa Hughes (D-Los Angeles), chair of the Assembly Education Committee.

authority to discipline; and raised teacher salaries.[6] The state superintendent of public instruction "crusaded relentlessly" for "new money and new attitudes."[7]

Increased Spending

New money came. By the start of the 1990s, government school spending per student, adjusted for inflation, had increased 40 percent since 1982 and had tripled since 1960.[8] (See Figure 3.1.) Does anyone seriously think the quality of government schooling tripled along with its cost?

There is no slowdown in sight. The National Center for Education Statistics estimates that nationwide spending for elementary and secondary education in 1993–94 will total $295.2 billion, or $5,920 per student.[9] Restated in terms of average daily attendance, rather than enrollment, that works out to $6,300 per student.[10] The United States now spends more on government education per student than any of its major economic competitors.[11] Thomas Sowell notes:

> We spend more money than Japan, for example, whether measured in real per-pupil expenditures or as a percentage of our gross national product. We have fewer pupils per class than Japan, and in mathematics our classes are less than half the size of Japanese math classes. The only thing we don't have are results.[12]

[6]Stephen Green, ed., *California Political Almanac* (Sacramento: California Journal Press, 1991), pp. 27, 50.

[7]Ibid., p. 49. State superintendent of public instruction Bill Honig also crusaded relentlessly for the Quality Education Project (QEP), an enterprise run by his wife, Nancy. The QEP received substantial state funds in violation of state ethics laws. Honig was indicted, convicted, and removed from office.

[8]On spending, see Joe Klein, "Conundrum in the Classroom," *Newsweek*, September 14, 1992, p. 32, citing a U.S. Department of Education report; Chubb and Moe, p. 101; Chuck Freadhoff, "Do Schools Need More Money?" *Investor's Daily*, September 20, 1991, pp. 1, 92; and Dana Wechsler, "Parkinson's Law 101," *Forbes*, June 25, 1990.

[9]Tamara Henry, "A New High for Education Spending," *USA Today*, September 3, 1993, p. 1D.

[10]Janet Novack, "What Do We Get for Our School Dollars?" *Forbes*, October 12, 1992, p. 92.

[11]*Wall Street Journal* news item, September 24, 1992, p. A1. See also John Hood, "Education: Is America Spending Too Much?" Cato Institute Policy Analysis no. 126, January 18, 1990; and John Hood, "Education: Money Isn't Everything," *Wall Street Journal*, February 9, 1990.

[12]Thomas Sowell, "Excuses, Excuses," *Forbes*, October 14, 1991, p. 43.

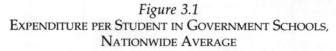

Figure 3.1
EXPENDITURE PER STUDENT IN GOVERNMENT SCHOOLS,
NATIONWIDE AVERAGE

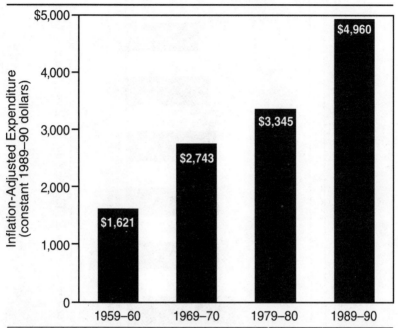

SOURCE: National Center for Education Statistics, Office of Educational Research and Improvement, U.S. Department of Education. *Digest of Education Statistics 1992* (NCES 92-097), p. 161.

The difference in funding is substantial. America spends 50 percent *more* per student than Japan, yet Japanese students consistently perform better.[13]

Only one nation, Switzerland, spends more per student on elementary and secondary education than the United States does. The United States outspends all others, including Germany, Japan, Britain, France, Sweden, the Netherlands, and Canada. (See Figure 3.2.)

Where Does All the Money Go?

America is getting less bang for its educational buck than its foreign competitors. We spend more money and get worse results. We are funding a government school system, but we are not funding

[13]"The Best Schools in the World," *Newsweek,* December 2, 1991, pp. 51–52.

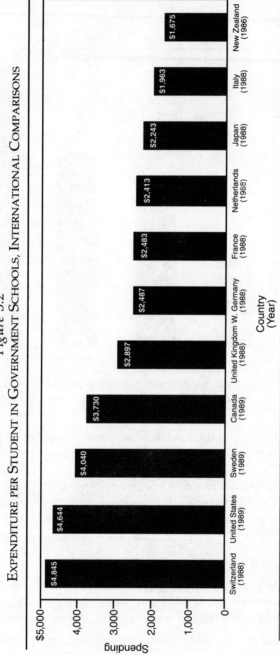

Figure 3.2
EXPENDITURE PER STUDENT IN GOVERNMENT SCHOOLS, INTERNATIONAL COMPARISONS

SOURCE: U.S. Department of Education, July 1992, cited in John Hood, "Righting the 'Rithmetic," *Reason,* January 1994.

much education. Much of the money ostensibly spent on the schools never reaches a classroom.

Let's take a closer look at how the largest state spends its educational dollars. As of fiscal year 1991–92, California was spending $28 billion attempting to educate 5.3 million students. The government school system costs California taxpayers about $5,242 per student per year.[14] Most taxpayers have no idea how expensive the system has become.[15]

Of the $3.9 billion spent by the Los Angeles Unified School District (LAUSD), *only 36 percent* trickles down to the classroom in the form of teacher salaries, textbooks, and supplies. How does LAUSD spend the remaining two-thirds of the money? For starters, 31 percent of the entire budget goes to nonschool-based administrative offices— the headquarters and the regional offices.[16] And how those offices spend the money is revealing. A few salaries for the 1990–91 school year:

Superintendent	$160,322
Deputy superintendent	143,243
Chief business and financial officer	143,243
Division administrator, business services	130,718

[14]Thomas W. Hayes, Director of Finance, State of California, wrote the following to state senator Bill Leonard in a letter dated September 24, 1991:

> Pursuant to your request, we have calculated a cost that includes every cost to state and local governments in maintaining elementary and secondary education for the 1991–92 fiscal year, but have not included costs associated with the unfunded liability for employee retirement benefits. That calculation sums all K–12 revenue sources, including the General Fund, federal funds, local property taxes, lottery funds, local debt service, and local miscellaneous income such as developer fees.

Total K–12 revenue	$28,021,500,000
1991–92 cost of STRS unfunded liability	− 275,708,000
	= 27,745,792,000
Unduplicated ADA [average daily attendance]	5,293,049

Scholarship at 100% = 5,242
Scholarship at 50% = 2,621.

[15]In a survey of 800 registered California voters, more than 60 percent of them underestimated spending, placing it at less than $4,000 per student per year. Arnold Steinberg and Anna David, "Summary Report: Survey of Voter Attitudes in California Toward a Choice System in Education," Reason Foundation Policy Insight no. 130, October 1991, pp. 1–2.

[16]Wayne Johnson, "Numbers Don't Lie; Fat Cats Do," *United Teacher*, February 9, 1990, p. 2.

Division administrator, building services	130,343
Division administrator, building services	128,208
Special counsel to the superintendent	127,729
Legal adviser	127,729

(In addition to employing both a special counsel and a legal adviser, LAUSD employs several assistant legal advisers. It also gives considerable legal work to high-priced outside counsel.)

Associate superintendent, government relations	$111,503
Division administrator, accounting services	110,746
Division administrator, financial services	110,746
Associate superintendent, personnel	109,004
Associate superintendent, school operator	108,579
Associate superintendent, instruction	108,579
Associate superintendent, technical support	108,579
Deputy administrator, business services	107,695
Assistant superintendent, senior high division	107,237
Assistant superintendent, elementary district	103,206
Assistant superintendent, information techician	103,206

(Four more assistant superintendents for elementary districts follow at $103,206 each, and another at $102,803.)

Assistant superintendent, special education	$102,803
Assistant superintendent, school-based management	102,803
Assistant superintendent, office of the superintendent	102,803

(An assistant superintendent just for the office of the superintendent?)

Personnel director	$102,803
Assistant superintendent, staff relations	102,803
Deputy director of information services	102,084
Secondary school teacher	100,780

Yes, one teacher makes over $100,000 annually. The district pays 31 employees over $100,000 per year; 133 employees over $90,000 per year; 607 employees over $80,000; 1,795 over $70,000; 6,052 over $60,000. Nearly 20,000 employees make more than $50,000 per year.[17]

[17]Sources: Los Angeles Unified School District budget; *Los Angeles Daily News* research. See "The Choice for LAUSD: Big Salaries or Big Classes," *Los Angeles Daily News*, August 15, 1991.

Los Angeles may seem like an extreme case, but it is not. Of all the people employed by California's government school system statewide, only 44 percent are teachers.[18] Put another way, for every 100 teachers in the government school system, there are 127 non-teachers. Some of them are driving buses and serving as guidance counselors, but what of the rest? Teaching children does not require that kind of bureaucracy. In fact, considerable evidence indicates that it only gets in the way.

In California's independent schools, on the other hand, fully 86 percent of the employees are teachers.[19] That figure includes special schools for physically and mentally challenged students. Obviously the government school system is spending a lot of tax dollars on activities other than teaching kids.

The story is the same around the country. In Milwaukee, 26 cents of every school dollar goes to teacher salaries, benefits, classroom supplies, textbooks, materials, and furniture. The balance—three-quarters of the entire budget—goes to maintenance, staff, administration, and transportation. In New York City, using the same criteria, 32.3 cents of every school dollar goes to the classroom.[20]

Not that teachers are poor. Nationally, the average government schoolteacher earns $36,000 annually for 185 days of work.[21] In California the average is over $40,000. In Los Angeles, the average teacher gets $44,500 for 180 days of work. Measured in conventional work-year terms, that translates to an annual salary rate of $55,625,[22] plus 22 percent of the average salary amount for benefit costs.[23]

They may be worth every penny. I personally favor compensating teachers well—as long as their pay is related to their performance, which it is presently not. My point is not that salaries are excessive, but that they are certainly adequate. In light of such salaries, and the far higher salaries for administrators, how can anyone blame the poor performance of the government school system on insufficient

[18]James S. Fay, ed., *California Almanac*, 5th ed. (Santa Barbara: Pacific Data Resources, 1991), p. 72.

[19]Ibid.

[20]Freadhoff, p. 1.

[21]Novack, p. 95.

[22]Lance Izumi, "California's Education System: Where Does All the Money Go?" Golden State Center for Policy Studies Briefing no. 1992–11, February 19, 1992, p. 6.

[23]Fay, pp. 73–74.

spending? "There is absolutely no evidence that higher spending produces higher student achievement," writes Janet Novack.[24]

In fact, much of the money already spent on schooling is wasted. Too much money is put into narrowly focused categorical programs, which are often built around the demands of special-interest groups and controlled by administrators at the top of the top-heavy system. These programs take money that should be spent on the academic basics. How much? In 1979–80, California's 25 then-existing categorical programs got $874 million. By 1990–91, over 80 separate categorical programs were swallowing a total of over $4 billion—an increase of over 450 percent. If a commensurate increase in test scores occurred, I missed it. Only 10 of those 80-plus programs arguably related to classroom instruction; in 1990–91, those 10 received a combined total of $509 million—less than 13 percent of the categorical budget.[25]

Where is the other 87 percent being spent? Here are the spending categories: administrator training and evaluation program, adult education, adults in correctional facilities, agricultural vocational education incentive program, alternative payment program, alternatives to school construction, alternatives to special education, American Indian education centers, apprentice programs, asbestos abatement, bilingual teacher training program, California child care initiative, California international studies project, California summer school for the arts, campus child care tax bailout, campus children's centers, child care resource and referral, child development, classroom teacher instructional improvement, class size reduction, committee on professional competence, court-ordered desegregation, deferred maintenance, demonstration program in reading and math, driver training, drug and alcohol abuse prevention program, economic impact aid/bilingual, educational technology program, emergency classrooms, environmental education, extended day care, foster youth services, general child development program, geography education, gifted and talented education, high school age parenting and infant development, high school pupil counseling, home to school transportation, institute of computer technology, instructional materials, intergenerational education, K–12 education staff

[24]Novack, p. 96.
[25]Izumi, pp. 7–16, 23–24.

development study, mentor teacher program, migrant day care, Miller-Unruh reading program, native American Indian early childhood education, native American Indian education program, new school construction, new teacher project, nutrition education and training project, opportunity classes and programs, partnership academies, peninsula academies model program, professional development program, protective services, pupil dropout prevention and recovery, reader service for blind teachers, regional occupational centers and program, regional science center, restructuring programs, SDE/ CSU minority underrepresentation and teacher improvement, school business personnel staff development, school improvement program, school/law enforcement partnership, school personnel staff development, small school district bus replacement, small school district transportation aid, special allowances for handicapped, special schools transportation, specialized secondary schools, specialized vocational educational program, state administration of special programs, state child nutrition program, state department of education administrative budget, state mandates, state preschool program, state special education clearinghouse depository, state special schools, support for local special education, summer school, teacher education and computer centers, teacher improvement program, urban impact aid, vocational education (state operations), vocational education student organizations, voluntary desegregation, and year-round school programs.[26]

This list, though exhausting, is not exhaustive; in addition to these categorical programs, the state provides general K–12 education support funding.[27] It also funds the state teacher retirement system. There are additional county and district programs. And I've listed only the program names. Listing the amount of spending on each would show that the more closely related a category is to teaching the academic basics, the less likely it is to receive substantial funding.

Some of these categories represent worthy causes, but are they really the job of a school? And if so, why must they be imposed by legislators and administered by bureaucrats in Sacramento and the county, district, and regional offices? Why can't the state simply provide base funding and trust people at the local level to provide education?

[26]Ibid., pp. 23–24; source, Legislative Analyst's Office.

[27]The statewide average base revenue limit is about $3,000.

Although these particular programs are from California, a similar morass is found in almost every state budget.

The Bottom Line: Results

Taxpayers probably wouldn't mind spending so much money if the students were obtaining what could reasonably be called an education. Voters probably wouldn't mind spending even more if there were reason to believe that that would help. On both counts, the educrats lose. Benno Schmidt again:

> Evidence of trouble in the schools has been growing for at least 20 years, and many devoted people have done a great deal to try to improve things. But evidence of real progress is hard to find. We have had ambitious national reform campaigns—from the post-Sputnik effort to breathe life into science and math programs and Great Society efforts to start education earlier and deal effectively with disadvantaged youngsters, to the greater academic focus and national standards movements of today—but progress has been marginal, at best.
>
> We have roughly doubled per-pupil spending (after inflation) in government schools since 1965; teachers have acquired more training; states have toughened high school graduation requirements. . . . [But] the nation's investment in educational improvement has produced very little return.[28]

In June 1993, the *Wall Street Journal* published a table comparing the government school systems of all states on the basis of three factors: annual cost per student, 1992 SAT scores, and 1992 eighth-grade NAEP scores. If there is any relationship between spending and achievement, it is an inverse one! Nationwide, average spending was $5,261 per student per year. New Jersey ranked first in spending ($9,159) but did rather poorly on test scores (14th on the NAEP; 39th on the SAT). Utah ranked last in spending by far ($2,993), but did very well on test scores (8th on the NAEP, 4th on the SAT). North Dakota ranked 46th in spending, but tied for 1st on the NAEP and came in 2nd on the SAT. Students in the highest spending states, in fact, ranked low academically, and students from several of the lowest spending states did relatively well.[29]

[28]Benno C. Schmidt, Jr., "Educational Innovation for Profit," *Wall Street Journal*, June 5, 1992, p. A12.

[29]Bruno V. Manno, "Deliver Us from Clinton's Schools Bill," *Wall Street Journal*, June 22, 1993, p. A14.

Who did best? Iowa ranked 1st on both the NAEP and the SAT—and ranked 30th in spending. California, which spent almost exactly the same amount as Iowa ($13 less per student) was 29th on the NAEP and 34th on the SAT. California educrats have a stable full of excuses, including illegal immigrants, bilingual education, and inner cities. New York has the same problems, but a number two ranking in spending ($8,500) hasn't solved them; New York was 22nd on the NAEP, 42nd on the SAT.[30]

Massachusetts ranked 8th in spending, 12th on the NAEP, and 33rd on the SAT. A team of economics professors at Suffolk University studied Massachusetts school districts, comparing dropout rates, SAT scores, and other criteria. Per-student spending had little relation to performance. The study team concluded, in essence, that more money would do little good without fundamental reform. Rather than increase funding, they recommended changing the way the schools were governed—particularly by offering parental choice.[31]

Spending more money on the government school system will not, by itself, improve performance. Chubb and Moe write:

> Indeed, researchers have generally been unable to establish a statistically significant relationship between student achievement and any of the school characteristics that are often thought important: teacher-pupil ratios, teacher education, teacher salaries, and per pupil expenditures....
>
> In fact, the relationship between resources and performance has been studied to death by social scientists, and their consistent conclusion has been that resources do not matter much, except perhaps in cases of extreme deprivation or gross abundance.[32]

Why hasn't more money resulted in better performance? Former secretary of education Bill Bennett bluntly asserts that the government school system

> now runs by-and-large for the sake of the people who run it rather than for the kids. I saw this dramatically illustrated more than once while I was education secretary. In 1986,

[30]Ibid.

[31]Patricia Mangan, "Ed Study: Money Is No Cure–All," *Boston Herald,* June 18, 1992, p. 8.

[32]Chubb and Moe, pp. 101, 193.

> California's Superintendent of Public Instruction Bill Honig
> was in my office at the Department of Education with Albert
> Shanker, president of the American Federation of Teachers.
> I had been pushing hard for choice and Honig said to me:
> give us five more years. If we don't dramatically improve
> education in five more years, I will be up in front of the
> parade with you arguing for choice. Well, the five years have
> passed and I have never heard from Honig, and California
> has not set records for educational achievement.[33]

Honig got what he asked for, more money and more time. The taxpayers got more excuses.

Eric Hanushek reviewed 60 studies attempting to link school expenditures to student achievement. He could find no relationship. "The conclusion that schools are operated in an economically inefficient manner has obvious implications for school policy," he writes. "The clearest one is simply that increased expenditures by themselves offer no overall promise for improving education. Further, the components of these expenditures offer little promise. Thus, a simple recommendation. Stop requiring and paying for things that do not matter."[34]

Conclusions

The government school system's poor performance cannot be blamed on political or societal indifference; during the past decade numerous reforms have been implemented with broad support. Nor can poor performance be blamed on financial neglect; the taxpayers have been generous. Spending on government education, adjusted for inflation and enrollment growth, has tripled over the last generation. America spends more per student than its chief international competitors—the ones thrashing us in academic comparisons. No evidence indicates that spending more money on the system will make it better.

Despite steady infusions of money, the system is producing deteriorating results. Isn't it time to ask what is wrong with the system?

---

[33]William J. Bennett, "An Obligation to Educate," *California Political Review*, Summer 1992, p. 21.

[34]Eric Hanushek, "The Economics of Schooling: Production and Efficiency in Public Schools," *Journal of Economic Literature* 24 (September 1986): 1167.

4. Why the System Resists Change, or the Rise of Centralization and the Decline of Everything Else

The Long-Sought Breakup of LAUSD

The Los Angeles Unified School District (LAUSD), within whose expansive boundaries I resided while serving as president of the Excellence through Choice in Education League (ExCEL), sprawls over 700 square miles and is theoretically educating 640,000 K–12 students. Board member Julie Korenstein recently made this remarkable discovery: "After being a member of the Board of Education for more than five years, I have come to the realization that this district is simply too big to be manageable, too entrenched with old bureaucratic ideas to be restructured and totally incapable of serving close to 1 million human beings."[1] Her discovery is remarkable only because parents have known that for years. Ms. Korenstein neglects to mention that her epiphany occurred after she ended up on the losing side of a reapportionment battle.

Korenstein proposes breaking the district into smaller, more manageable entities. It's a good idea, but if you think LAUSD is going quietly, I've got some oceanfront property in Arizona for you. I've also got an interesting piece of historical memorabilia: *Educational Renewal: A Decentralization Proposal for the Los Angeles Unified School District*, prepared by the Decentralization Task Force, dated February 22, 1971. Volume I, the summary, contains 159 pages of unimplemented recommendations to rearrange the deck chairs on the *Titanic*. Task forces of one kind or another have been recommending that LAUSD decentralize for years. The latest decentralization plan comes from LEARN, the Los Angeles Educational Alliance for

[1] Julie Korenstein, "Stop the District—We Want Off," *Los Angeles Times*, August 20, 1992, p. B13.

Restructuring Now. A more appropriate name would be LEARSDF, the Los Angeles Educational Alliance for Restructuring Someday in the Distant Future. The LAUSD bureaucracy resists decentralization and vehemently opposes breakup, apparently on the theory that as long as they're losing money they should try to make it up in volume.

Any decentralization plan that leaves the district bureaucracy intact is bound to fail. Thus, for decades, bolder reformers have been trying to divide LAUSD into smaller districts. The attempt that came closest to success was in the form of a bill cosponsored by Assemblyman Bill Greene (D-Watts), a former field representative for the Congress of Racial Equality, and Sen. John L. Harmer (R-Glendale), my father. Working with an alliance of minority liberals and white conservatives, Harmer succeeded in pushing the bill through both houses of the legislature—only to have then-governor Ronald Reagan veto it on September 20, 1970, for reasons still unknown.[2]

The latest convert to the cause is state senate president pro tem David A. Roberti (D-Van Nuys). Like Ms. Korenstein's, Roberti's conversion occurred in the wake of reapportionment, when he suddenly found himself courting new constituents in the San Fernando Valley. Although in 1970 he voted against the Harmer bill, in 1993 he became a champion of breakup, having discovered that his new constituents were "fed up with a public school 'behemoth that gets bigger and bigger' but cannot seem to educate students or allow parents a voice."[3] Roberti asks, "How can parents be involved if they travel an hour and a half in traffic from Van Nuys to [LAUSD headquarters] downtown?"[4] How indeed. Roberti's bill would divide LAUSD into seven still massive districts. He promoted the plan vigorously as a way to stave off the dreaded Parental Choice in Education Initiative, which would have let kids escape from LAUSD schools altogether.[5]

Roberti's discovery of the evils of centralization is recent, but the evils themselves are not. Introducing his breakup bill in 1968, Senator

[2]Ralph Frammolino, "Breaking Up's Been Hard to Do," *Los Angeles Times*, May 16, 1993, p. A1.

[3]Ibid.

[4]Ibid.

[5]Mark Gladstone, "School Choice Initiative Boosts Other Reform Plans," *Los Angeles Times*, June 1, 1993, p. A1.

Harmer spoke of LAUSD's "poor community support, poor teaching and poor education." He added, "The Los Angeles School Board, by its own admission, has acknowledged these problems and has attributed them to the district's enormous size." Harmer's bill would have created 10 new districts of about 65,000 students each.[6] LAUSD, of course, opposed it.

The East Germans built a wall to keep unwilling subjects in; LAUSD uses lawyers. Among the neighborhoods trying to secede from LAUSD is the Eastview area of Rancho Palos Verdes, which wants to join the closer and better Palos Verdes Peninsula Unified School District. LAUSD lawyers have been blocking Eastview for five years. Every time the Eastview citizens have won any legal approval, LAUSD has appealed it. The state board of education finally rejected LAUSD's so-called final appeal, so Eastview scheduled a secession vote—and LAUSD sued again![7]

Stop for a moment and think of the tax money spent on those lawsuits. I used to practice law, and I know how it works: if you sneeze, you bill the client for 15 minutes of your time plus a box of Kleenex. The tax dollars wasted on legal bills generated by LAUSD's refusal to let people escape could have purchased a lot of textbooks.

The One Best System

Centralization is not unique to LAUSD; it is what the modern government school system is all about. In 1945 there were over 100,000 government school districts nationwide.[8] Today there are fewer than 15,000.[9] In the old days, local school boards ran the schools and teachers ran the classrooms; parents retained ultimate authority, and they knew where to go to complain. Today state legislators and state educrats preempt vast areas of school policy and procedure; school boards have the authority to do what the state tells them. Superintendents and principals are middle managers,

[6]"Bill Proposes 10-Part L.A. School District," *Los Angeles Times*, February 10, 1968, Part I, p. 3.

[7]Ronald B. Taylor, "L.A. Unified Will Sue to Block Eastview Secession Vote," *Los Angeles Times*, June 19, 1992, p. B3.

[8]Steven Hayward, "Reforming Education: A Primer on School Choice," Pacific Research Institute briefing paper. Undated; issued in 1992.

[9]National Center for Education Statistics, *Digest of Education Statistics 1993* (Washington: NCES, 1993), Table 88.

and teachers have little autonomy left. For parents, changing school policy in some areas is no easier than changing the state budget.

I am the oldest of 10 children. We come from the same parents, we were raised in the same environment, and we were taught the same values, but we are as unique and individual as can be. Sometimes we wonder whether our brother Chris and our sister Betsy are members of the same species, let alone the same family. Mom and Dad understand that on some matters each of us requires a different approach.

If such differences occur in a single cohesive family, imagine the diversity of the human beings one finds in a single classroom. Multiply those differences again and again, and imagine the infinite variety of children in a statewide government school system, each a unique individual with unique possibilities and unique needs. Imposing a one-size-fits-all system on those children and expecting it to work is the height of folly, but that is what we have done. The system is a monolithic monopoly with very little local flexibility. Rather than shaping the system city by city and school by school and class by class to fit the children, we expect the children to fit the system.

Like so many other maladies, including the federal income tax, the "one best system" comes from the Progressive Era, when, in the words of David Boaz,

> the best-educated Americans believed that experts armed with social science and goodwill—and power—could make decisions about all sorts of social institutions that would be implemented by government to benefit all Americans. The Progressives were not socialists, but the one best system was essentially socialist in nature. Obviously it was intended to be one system for the whole society, centrally directed and bureaucratically managed, with little use for competition or market incentives.[10]

The obvious winners in such a system were the education professionals. The losers, write Chubb and Moe, were

> the lower classes, ethnic and religious minorities, and citizens of rural communities. Their traditional control over local

[10]David Boaz, "The Public School Monopoly: America's Berlin Wall," in *Liberating Schools: Education in the Inner City*, ed. David Boaz (Washington: Cato Institute, 1991), p. 12.

schools was now largely transferred to the new system's political and administrative authorities—who, according to what soon became official doctrine, knew best what kind of education people needed and how it could be provided most effectively.[11]

I once saw a cartoon in which a tall, slender, male obstetrician was telling a very uncomfortable woman, apparently in the 10th month of her pregnancy, "There, there, Mrs. Jones—I know exactly how you feel." The look on her face said: the hell you do. Turning education over to the so-called experts is like that. What do the experts know that parents and teachers don't? Nothing, says one veteran teacher: "Experts in education have never been right; their 'solutions' are expensive, self-serving, and always involve further centralization. We've seen the results."[12] He adds:

> If we use schooling to break children away from parents—and make no mistake, that has been the central function of schools since John Cotton announced it as the purpose of the Bay Colony schools in 1650 and Horace Mann announced it as the purpose of Massachusetts schools in 1850—we're going to continue to have the horror show we have right now.[13]

School choice empowers and includes parents, rather than replaces them. It allows for the development of schools and classes and methods as varied as the children they serve. Parents seem to like the idea. The "experts" don't.

Denial

From January 26 to 29, 1993, I attended the annual Superintendents Symposium of the Association of California School Administrators (ACSA). The welcome letter from the convention chairman alleged that "severe budget cuts" faced the schools, but somehow they found the money to put everyone up at the Hyatt Regency in Monterey. In between sightseeing trips and banquets, ACSA's leadership

---

[11]John E. Chubb and Terry M. Moe, *Politics, Markets and America's Schools* (Washington: Brookings Institution, 1990), p. 4.

[12]John Taylor Gatto, *Dumbing Us Down* (Philadelphia: New Society Publishers, 1992), p. 38.

[13]Ibid., p. 37.

announced an alarming erosion of public support for the schools, which they linked to the campaign for the Parental Choice in Education Initiative. "Most Californians are out of touch with today's schools," ACSA executive director Wes Apker said without a hint of irony. ACSA, characteristically, had decided to respond with a multiyear media campaign that would attempt to persuade the public that the schools were doing a great job but that they needed more money.[14] The ACSA members gave Apker thunderous applause.[15]

ACSA's decision to combat mediocre government school performance with a public relations campaign reminded me of another conference I had attended shortly before. On November 17, 1992, the Fresno Chamber of Commerce hosted the annual Valley Education Conference. The keynote speaker, Dr. David Berliner, said, "Educators haven't failed society; society has failed educators." That was what the attendees wanted to hear. Berliner charged that perceptions of poor government school performance were grossly inaccurate. Then why were those perceptions so pervasive? He said, and I promise this is a direct quote, "It is a conspiracy. The right wing has to discredit American schools to put a voucher system into place."[16]

One more experience. On March 5, 1992, I attended a prebreakfast meeting of the San Bernardino Chamber of Commerce. I had been told that chamber members would listen to supporters and opponents of the Parental Choice in Education Initiative and then consider whether to take a position. As it turned out, the chamber's education committee, which included several government school officials, had already decided to oppose the initiative. They packed the meeting; the majority of attendees, I later learned, were members of the school board, the district bureaucracy, and the teachers union—hardly the usual Chamber of Commerce crowd. I should have suspected foul

[14]The nature of the welcome given visiting politicians depended exclusively on whether they shared this view. Those who wanted huge increases in school spending were heroes, and those who wanted modest increases were public enemies. Among the former was state superintendent of public instruction Bill Honig. Notwithstanding his impending conviction and removal from office, he got a standing ovation. There were tears on some faces. When Gov. Pete Wilson came to speak, no one stood and no one cried. The ACSA leadership vacated the dais, refusing to appear with him.

[15]I know this seems too funny to be true, but it is true. I have a complete copy of ACSA's accompanying media kit, as does every significant reporter in California.

[16]Again, this may seem too ridiculous to be true, but a transcript will confirm my detailed notes of the event.

play when the chair opened the question-and-answer session by saying, "Now please remember that Mr. Harmer is our guest and this is just an information-gathering session."

After the debate I offered my hand to my opponent, the school superintendent; he responded with verbal abuse. It was one of the nastier moments of the campaign. Contrary to what the chair had promised, she took a vote, which went against the initiative. Every businessperson present favored school choice. Several of them spoke of their children who had witnessed or personally experienced violence in the government schools. They were outnumbered by the education establishment, however.

I had spoken about the importance of teaching children; the superintendent had spoken only about preserving the system. At the ACSA convention, the Valley Education Conference, the San Bernardino meeting, and dozens more where I have spoken, the assumption is always the same: We already have the one best system; give it more money and keep your hands off it. The experts have a monopoly on tax money earmarked for education. They want to keep it that way.

Competition and Consequences

After we were married, my wife Elayne took my name, which necessitated a visit to the Social Security office. It was a miserable experience, of course. We entered a large, stale-smelling room where row after row of people were sitting in folding chairs, all facing a massive wall with half a dozen small windows in it. Everyone looked numb. A clerk yelled, "Fourteen!" and someone walked to the window. Elayne and I looked for the numbers, took one, and sat down. Our number was 73. "Fifteen!" an agent yelled a minute later.

"This is ridiculous," Elayne sputtered. "All I have to do is turn in this form. We shouldn't have to wait." She walked to a couple of the windows and was rebuffed at each. The Social Security Administration insisted that she appear in person, and she was going to have to wait her turn. It reminded us of government offices we had visited in Third World countries. (Elayne was born in South America, and both of us had lived there for several years.)

The clerks proceeded at a languorous pace. An hour after we arrived, one of them finally called our number. It took less than a minute to handle the transaction, and at long last we were on our way.

We had several other errands to run that day. The department store had exactly what we needed. The bank handled our transaction promptly. The sandwich shop served good food, cheerfully. The supermarket had competitive prices and good service. Each business gave us what we wanted in pleasant surroundings at a fair price and promptly.

What a contrast to the government office! Why the difference? Freedom and competition. If Elayne and I found poor service at one store, bank, restaurant, market, or any other enterprise, we would go to a different one. There are all sorts of alternatives, and we can choose freely among them. No stores can compel us to patronize them; either they meet our needs or they lose our business. Not even the largest business is more powerful than the consumer. If mighty GM sells dull cars that fall apart, customers start buying Toyotas and bring the corporation to its knees. If legendary IBM isn't as quick as its competitors, then the competitors get the business. And the customer wins. Seller beware! In a free market you satisfy the customer or you go broke. The business pages are full of companies learning that humbling lesson.

It is a lesson no government enterprise ever learns, because government shields itself from competition. Elayne and I have to pay our substantial Social Security taxes even though the Social Security Administration treats us like nuisances, and even though we would prefer to prepare for retirement by investing more profitably elsewhere.

Like the Social Security Administration and other government bureaucracies, government schools get our money and our children regardless of how they perform and regardless of whether we find other alternatives preferable. A few parents can afford independent schools, and a rapidly growing number are choosing to do the job themselves through home schooling, but most parents have no choice. The government takes their tax dollars and promises to educate their children. If government fails to deliver, what recourse do the parents have? None. The ponderous government school bureaucracy is insulated from competition, and it changes at a glacial pace.

Protected from competition, government school personnel face no meaningful consequences for success or failure. Does great teaching result in higher salaries or more autonomy? No. Does poor teaching result in getting fired or losing pay? No. The National Education

Association (NEA), the largest teachers union, adamantly opposes merit pay and has thwarted most attempts to institute it.

Competition spurs the imitation of success. Monopoly allows the perpetuation of failure. Insulated from competition, given a monopoly over the tax-funded education of children, is it any wonder that the government school system performs so poorly? The need for measurement, competition, and consequences "should be a strong argument in favor of giving parents the widest possible choice of where to send their kids," writes *Newsweek's* Joe Klein. But the education establishment opposes that idea. American Federation of Teachers president Al Shanker is "vehemently opposed," and Shanker

> —whose vision and flexibility tend to evaporate when the jobs of his union's members are at stake—is light years ahead of the leadership at the other big teachers' union, the National Education Association, which opposes anything that smacks of accountability and has lobbied not only against choice but also against standards and testing.[17]

The Bias against Excellence

The government school system's insulation from competition fosters an ambivalent attitude toward academic excellence. Excellence rarely if ever arises from ease; but the system's aversion to the challenge of the market is reflected in its reluctance to challenge its students. So egalitarian is today's government school system that it refuses to discriminate not only on the grounds of race, creed, color, and sex, but also on the grounds of ability, effort, behavior, performance, quality, moral worth, and merit. Bemoaning the "pervasive dumbing-down of the curriculum," Daniel J. Singal writes:

> Consider the teaching of English. The Great Books, of course, are out of fashion. . . . Feed a student the literary equivalent of junk food and you will get an impoverished command of English, which is what we too often see in the current crop of college freshmen. . . .
>
> Perhaps most crucial, the sixties mentality, with its strong animus against what it defines as "elitism," has shifted the locus of concern in American education from high to low achievers. . . . The prevailing ideology holds that it is much better to give up the prospect of excellence than to take

[17]Joe Klein, "Conundrum in the Classroom," *Newsweek*, September 14, 1992, p. 32.

the chance of injuring any student's self-esteem. . . . These attitudes have become so ingrained that in conversations with teachers and administrators one often senses a virtual prejudice against bright students.[18]

Aside from alleged underfunding, the education establishment blames television, rock music, single-parent families, and general social maladies for its poor performance. Singal thinks other factors—such as the reluctance to group students by aptitude and performance and the failure to focus on academic basics—are more likely explanations. After all, nothing in the effective schools' literature indicates that effective schools had to banish television, rock music, children of single parents, or social maladies before improving.

Strong Unions, Weak Reforms

Given the increased funding and the reform efforts of the 1980s, why hasn't government school performance improved? For one thing, many reforms were blocked or undercut by the education establishment. More fundamentally, though, the reforms leave the government school system's monopoly intact. The consumer choice that drives progress in every other field is denied to parents. As long as parents lack affordable alternatives to the government school system, the schools won't have to change.

Jackie Ducote, executive vice president of the Louisiana Association of Business and Industry, is typical of many in the business community who have reached the same conclusion. At first she was optimistic that, with business support, the present government school system would improve. Not anymore:

> In 1987, the Louisiana Association of Business and Industry took stock of its reform efforts and issued a report called "10 Years of Education Reform in Louisiana: A Long Journey to Nowhere." Most reforms had been watered down, ignored, not implemented properly, taken to court by the teacher unions and others, mired in turf battles or not funded.
>
> In 1988, our new governor, Buddy Roemer, pushed through another batch of reforms that seem headed for a similar fate. Both teacher unions have filed suits to gut the

[18]Daniel J. Singal, "The Other Crisis in American Education," *Atlantic Monthly*, November 1991, pp. 66–67.

teacher accountability provisions of his package, tied to a 30 percent pay raise. True to form, the unions waited until after they received the final installment of the pay raise before filing suit.

Piecemeal attempts to change the present system haven't worked and won't work because the present system is a monopoly. It has a captive clientele and guaranteed funding regardless of results. Thus, it has no incentive to change, and parents and students have no leverage. They can't take their business elsewhere unless they are willing and able to pay twice for it.[19]

The teachers unions are the largest single obstacle to meaningful reform. With 2.1 million members, NEA is not only the largest teachers union, but the largest union of any kind in the United States, larger than the Teamsters. Most teachers, in order to join a local education association, must also join the NEA and its state affiliate. Membership dues are staggering—about $400 a year.[20] With the possible exception of the post office, schools are the most heavily unionized places in the country. Obviously, that gives the NEA a great deal of power; as Peter Brimelow and Leslie Spencer note, it is "the near-monopoly supplier" of labor to "a government-enforced monopoly consumer."[21]

Lamar Alexander, who knows from experience as governor of Tennessee, says, "Only a very determined governor has the influence to marshal enough power to overcome [NEA state affiliate] opposition."[22] In many states, the teachers union is the largest single lobby and one of the largest political donors. Such is the case in California. During 1991 the California Teachers Association (CTA), the NEA affiliate, spent $2,616,845 lobbying the legislature—more than any other organization. The CTA ranked ahead of the insurance industry, the oil industry, the California Medical Association, the California Manufacturers Association, and even the California Trial Lawyers Association.[23] In 1992 the CTA donated $374,522 to candidates for

[19]Jackie Ducote, "Confessions of an Education-Reform Junkie," *Wall Street Journal*, December 14, 1990.

[20]Peter Brimelow and Leslie Spencer, "The National Extortion Association?" *Forbes*, June 7, 1993, p. 79.

[21]Ibid. p. 80.

[22]Ibid., p. 74.

[23]Information obtained from the office of the California Secretary of State.

state office—an amount exceeded only by the California Medical PAC and the Democratic State Central Committee.[24] Nationwide, the NEA's political action committee raised $6.5 million in 1992 alone.[25]

Having frustrated past reforms, the NEA is now turning its guns on school choice proposals. The New Jersey affiliate is taking aim at Bret Schundler, the new mayor of Jersey City, who is determined to provide parental choice in education. Schundler, who may be the only Republican in Jersey City, won an amazing 69 percent of the vote on a platform favoring school choice. Jersey City spends $9,240 per year per student on its government schools, which have a drop-out rate of 60 percent. Many of the 40 percent who do graduate are functionally illiterate. Meanwhile, 25 percent of school-age children in Jersey City attend Catholic schools that, for one-third the cost, graduate 90 percent of their students. "The teachers unions aren't afraid we'll fail," Mayor Schundler says. "They're afraid we'll succeed."[26]

If the government school monopoly ends, so does much of the NEA's power. Thus its opposition to school choice. In California, the NEA/CTA not only opposed the Parental Choice in Education Initiative, it did everything possible to keep the initiative off the ballot. Its heavy-handed tactics took negative campaigning in California to a new low, a story detailed in Chapter 8.

Knowing Little, Feeling Fine

Why does the CTA fear a system in which parents would be free to choose alternatives? Perhaps because many CTA members aren't teaching much. Author Rita Kramer spent a year crisscrossing the country visiting colleges of education and observing how they train government schoolteachers. It was a distressing experience:

> Almost nowhere did I find teachers of teachers whose emphasis was on the measurable learning of real knowledge. The aim is not to produce individuals capable of effort and mastery but to make sure everyone gets a passing grade. The school is to be remade into a republic of feelings—as distinct from a republic of learning—where everyone can feel he deserves an A.

[24]Paul Jacobs, "Doctors, Teachers Union among Top Political Donors," *Los Angeles Times*, September 15, 1992, p. A27.

[25]Brimelow and Spencer, p. 74.

[26]"The NEA's Public Enemy #1," *Wall Street Journal*, July 13, 1993, p. A14.

> What matters is not to teach any particular subject or skill,
> not to preserve past accomplishments or stimulate future
> achievements, but to give to all that stamp of approval that
> will make them "feel good about themselves." Self-esteem
> has replaced understanding as the goal of education.[27]

For vivid evidence of the pervasiveness of this problem, see *The First Year of Teaching*, a highly acclaimed book of essays on life in the classroom.[28] Some of the stories are heartwarming, but others make you wonder. Several stories tell of so-called students who finished their grade unable to read, even students who finished *high school* unable to read, but the writers note cheerfully that their self-confidence was undiminished. One teacher counsels others not to tie their own self-esteem to their students' performance; it might be depressing. One essay lauds some graduating students whose crowning academic achievement appears to have been learning a Whitney Houston song. Most remarkable of all, none of the contributors entertains the idea that something is wrong with the system that compels kids to come but lets them leave so poorly prepared.

The System Is the Problem

John Taylor Gatto, New York State's teacher of the year for 1991, says, "It is the great triumph of compulsory government monopoly mass-schooling that among even the best of my fellow teachers, and among even the best of my students' parents, only a small number can imagine a different way to do things."[29] Among those unable to imagine a different way were most of the reformers of the 1980s, whose work did nothing to alter the present system's monopoly. The reforms all occurred within the existing system, writes David Kearns, "leaving a residue of incremental changes and an outmoded educational structure still firmly in place."[30] *Education Week* quotes another critic: "I don't think we've gotten to the heart of the problem. We're still talking about testing everybody and putting the screws on the existing system even more. The problem is the existing system.

[27]Rita Kramer, "School Daze," *Reason*, May 1992, p. 25, 31.

[28]Pearl Rock Kane, ed., *The First Year of Teaching* (New York: Mentor, 1992).

[29]Gatto, p. 12.

[30]Quoted by Joseph Murphy, "The Educational Reform Movement of the 1980s: A Comprehensive Analysis," in *The Educational Reform Movement of the 1980s*, ed. Joseph Murphy (Berkeley, Calif.: McCutchan Publishing Corp., 1990), p. 25.

And until we face up to that unpleasant fact—that the existing system has to change—we're not going to get the kinds of changes that everybody wants.[31]

"Existing institutions cannot solve the problem," Chubb and Moe agree, "because they *are* the problem." Indeed, under the present monopoly, "poor performance is just as much a normal, enduring part of the political landscape as school boards and superintendents are."[32] Chubb and Moe reached their conclusions after taking the most comprehensive database on American schools and augmenting it with the Administrator and Teacher Survey, giving them "the best empirical foundation currently available for exploring the environment, organization, and performance of schools." They "sifted through hundreds of variables, keeping some (220 to be exact)." Their exhaustive research revealed three general principles:

First, effective schools shared the same characteristics: clear goals, ambitious academic programs, strong leadership, and high levels of teacher professionalism. This was no surprise; several other studies had identified similar characteristics. But Chubb and Moe went further, seeking to discover what caused some schools to develop those characteristics.

Second, "the most important prerequisite for the emergence of effective school characteristics is school autonomy, especially from external bureaucratic influence." In other words, the harder you try to *compel* schools to have clear goals, ambitious academic programs, and so on, the harder it is for the schools to actually develop them. To develop these characteristics, what schools need most is to be left alone. They need freedom. Legislative mandates and bureaucratic controls only get in the way.

Third, "America's existing system of public education inhibits the emergence of effective organizations." This occurs because the system is governed by political institutions, which "function naturally to limit and undermine school autonomy."[33] In other words, the hardest thing for any governmental body to do is to refrain from exercising authority. If a political entity has authority over the

---

[31]Theodore R. Sizer, quoted in L. Olson, "Reform: Plaudits for Staying Power, Prescriptions for New Directions," *Education Week* 7, no. 32 (1988): 1, 21; quoted in turn by Murphy, p. 25.

[32]Chubb and Moe, pp. 2–3; emphasis in original.

[33]Ibid., pp. 22–23.

schools, it will inevitably exercise that authority; and to the extent that it does, it will limit school autonomy—the very prerequisite for improvement.

An independent school has a clear clientele: the parents! The independent school operator does whatever it takes to satisfy them, or they take their students out. The government schools, in contrast, "are not in the business of pleasing parents and students, and they cannot be allowed to set their own agendas. Their agendas are set by politicians, administrators, and the various democratic constituencies that hold the keys to political power."[34] Chubb and Moe consider the implications for four key areas of school management: personnel, goals, leadership, and practice.

In personnel matters, the government school principal has little control over who works at the school and how they are compensated. Laws and regulations strictly govern certification, hiring, collective bargaining, tenure, and other aspects of personnel management. For the teachers unions, "the notion that rewards might somehow be linked to merit is anathema."[35] Thus, the principal is severely constrained in his or her wish to hire and reward good teachers, and fire or reduce the rewards of poor ones. Many of the important qualities the principal seeks in teachers—enthusiasm, collegiality, communication skills, creativity, special sensitivity to student problems—cannot be measured (although they can be perceived), and thus cannot be used in evaluations.[36]

Government schools cannot set their own goals; the entire state education code and accompanying regulations, which may take several feet of shelf space, are their goals. They have to follow the entire body of laws. The sheer volume of those mandates is overwhelming, and there is no clear coherence, structure, or priority to them.[37]

The government school principal is not free to lead; he has to manage. His role consists chiefly of implementing policy made by others.

Finally, with regard to practice, "in the public sector, the whole thrust of democratic politics is to formalize and constrain educational practice. As public authority is captured and put to use by various

[34]Ibid., p. 38.
[35]Ibid., p. 48.
[36]Ibid., p. 50.
[37]Ibid., p. 54.

interests over time, the discretionary exercise of professional judgment is systematically curtailed, and the practice of education is transformed into an exercise in administration."[38]

Chubb and Moe conclude that the government school reforms of the 1980s have not improved, and will not improve, government school performance because the old institutions of political control remain in place. They predict that significant improvement will not occur until parents are free to choose among schools and schools are free to compete for students.[39]

The Need for Choice

Schools exist primarily to teach the academic basics. The government school system is doing a poor job of it. The system's poor performance persists despite a decade of reform and substantially increased funding. The system resists improvement. It is highly centralized and thus unable to adapt itself to the infinite diversity and variety of children it is supposed to serve. It is managed by bureaucrats whose self-interest prevents them from even admitting, much less addressing, its failings. It is dominated by unions that aggressively promote their own interests. And most fundamental of all, it is governed through political authority rather than free individual choices.

The school system is a government-owned, government-operated monopoly. Most children must attend the school within whose boundaries they reside, regardless of its quality. Payment for the product is automatic, regardless of the individual consumer's satisfaction with the service. "Such a unified, centralized system is a dinosaur in the information age," writes David Boaz.[40] Government schools have few direct incentives to excel and almost no penalty for failure.

Outside the education establishment, there is broad agreement that the fundamental problem is the system itself, and that improvement requires removing authority from the centralized bureaucracy and restoring it to the local level. For major improvement, we need

[38]Ibid., p. 58.
[39]Ibid., p. 228.
[40]Boaz, p. 13.

to give principals freedom to lead; give teachers freedom to teach; give schools freedom to compete for students; and, most important, give parents the freedom to choose among schools.

5. Independent School Performance

Some government schools do a splendid job. (I was fortunate to attend one of them.) Examples of outstanding teachers and principals abound—Jaime Escalante in California, Marva Collins in Chicago, John Taylor Gatto in New York. Dozens of books and studies analyze government school success stories—many of them in trying circumstances, with low funds and large classes. As David Barulich has observed, "The problem in public education is not a lack of knowledge of what works. The problem is that very few people are taking action to emulate what works."[1]

"Alternative" Schools

An amusing example of the Barulich Doctrine is the charter schools bill California enacted in 1992. State senator Gary Hart, the bill's author, "envisions the proposed 'charter' schools as those where only the academic basics are taught," reported the *Los Angeles Times*.[2] Teaching the academic basics—now that's a novel idea. What are the other government schools teaching?

"We are trying to break out of the bureaucratic, legalistic mode that is so frustrating to so many people," Hart told the *Times*. Yet the Hart bill is itself full of bureaucratic legalities, the primary one being a strict limit on the number of charter schools. No more than 100 can be created, in a state with 5.3 million government school students.[3] That works out to a maximum of one charter school for every 53,000 students. Want to guess your child's chances of getting in? Senator Hart and his allies in the education establishment apparently have no problem with a two-tier system in which an elite group of 100 schools can exclude most students.

[1]Personal letter to author, October 15, 1992.

[2]Carl Ingram, "Governor Signs Legislation to Allow 'Charter' Schools," *Los Angeles Times*, September 22, 1992, p. A3.

[3]Ibid.

Another example: the Lincoln Alternative School in Corona, California. What is "alternative" about Lincoln? "The school was formed 11 years ago," reports the *Corona Independent*, "by people who wanted an elementary school that emphasized homework, had a rigorous discipline policy and a strict dress code. Lincoln emphasizes patriotism and the three R's." If that is "alternative," is it any wonder that the government school system performs poorly?

Every year, parents camp in the parking lot outside the Corona-Norco Unified School District headquarters, some arriving over 48 hours before registration begins, to try to get their children into such a school. "School board trustees are quick to point out that the same values are important in all of the district's schools."[4] Then why are parents spending the weekend in their sleeping bags on a parking lot just to get their children in? More importantly, why aren't the other schools imitating Lincoln's obviously successful program?

At the opposite end of the country, the school district in Arlington, Virginia, also offers alternative schools emphasizing reading, writing, and arithmetic.[5] Reading, writing, and arithmetic are alternatives? To what?

The problem isn't figuring out what works; to the parents camping out for registration at places like the Lincoln School, and even to the legislators who favor charter schools, that is obvious. The problem is figuring out how to get the government school system to *do* what works. At times the system seems more interested in penalizing excellence than in encouraging it. While serving as secretary of education, Bill Bennett

> went to miraculous places where people were turning things around, like Garfield High School in Los Angeles where Jaime Escalante was teaching. He's gone from Garfield now. This great teacher—the greatest teacher in America, maybe the greatest teacher in the world—is now in Sacramento because the unions couldn't deal with his methods. He had 75 students in his class and some of his colleagues said union rules say you can have only 22.3 students in your class. He said fine, you take some of them and teach them calculus.

[4]Craig Van Rooyen, "Camp-Out Becomes Traditional," *Corona Independent*, March 18, 1992, p. A1.

[5]David Boaz, "The Public School Monopoly: America's Berlin Wall," in *Liberating Schools: Education in the Inner City*, ed. David Boaz (Washington: Cato Institute, 1991), p. 28.

They said we don't know calculus. He said then get out of my way and let me teach.

It is encouraging to go to a school like that, where kids who come in with almost nothing leave blessed by their schools, by their teachers, by their principals. They can read. They are interested and want to go on. When you see it actually happening, you are encouraged. You know it's possible. When people say you cannot educate these kids, you know they are wrong. It is being done in American schools, but it is not being done in most American schools.

It is *discouraging* to go then into schools with essentially the same kids, in the same kind of neighborhoods, and see lousy education going on . . . when you see that kids *can* learn, that schools can make a mighty and dramatic difference in their lives, then you get angry about it.[6]

"Angry" is right. Disadvantaged children aren't an abstraction; they are our neighbors and they deserve better. Look at them. Look at their schools. Are they getting the education they need? For that matter, look at comfortable middle-class children. Their schools may be safer but they, too, are grossly undereducated. We have paused on the plateau of educational mediocrity for too long. We know how to do much better.

Exceptional Schools

Excellent schools already exist, even in the toughest surroundings. For example, while other kids are doing time in the inner-city government schools, look what happens at the Marcus Garvey School, as reported by economist Walter Williams:

Dr. Amyin Parker founded the Marcus Garvey school in South Central Los Angeles in 1975. If you visited, you'd see 2-year-olds reciting the ABC's, 3-year-olds counting in English, Spanish, and Swahili and 4-year-olds doing math. Down the hall, in Miss Brenda Spencer's English class, you'd hear second-graders spelling words like pharmaceutical, entrepreneur, and cerebellum. And if that surprises you, the same kids might recite Abraham Lincoln's Gettysburg address from memory and do elementary algebra. Or you could listen in on Miss Vanessa Beverly's fourth-grade class, where the kids learn the periodic table. . . . Farther down the

[6]William J. Bennett, "An Obligation to Educate," *California Political Review,* Summer 1992, pp. 20–21; transcript of extemporaneous speech; emphasis in original.

hall, you'd see Alfonso Thrower teaching math, including elementary differential calculus, to fifth- and sixth-graders.

Marcus Garvey is not a rich white suburban school. It's a black school with 400 students located at 2916 W. Slauson Ave. in a troubled section of Los Angeles. Its students are not gifted. They are ordinary kids, with concerned parents, going to an extraordinary school with black administrators and teachers who have unbounded pride and a sense of mission.[7]

The magazine *Urban Family* reports on the effect such high expectations had on one Marcus Garvey student:

> When Jovan English got her grades back early this summer, she was disappointed that she only achieved B's in her two most important classes, calculus and analytic geometry. Her grades were average in relation to her classmates at the University of California at Los Angeles, but Jovan wasn't satisfied.
>
> Sound familiar? Hardly. Jovan is a 12-year-old eighth grader at Marcus Garvey School in South Central Los Angeles and takes a couple of courses at UCLA on the side.
>
> At Garvey, Jovan is an exception, but not by far.[8]

Marcus Garvey achieves this success at a tuition cost of $3,200 per year—about 60 percent of the state school system's $5,200 per-pupil cost. If Marcus Garvey can deliver immeasurably better results at less than two-thirds the price, isn't something wrong with the government school system? Cost aside, why aren't government schools imitating what works so well at Marcus Garvey?

Superb schools like Marcus Garvey are scattered throughout the country. One of them is Marva Collins's Westside Preparatory School in Chicago. There, three-year-old students read at the third-grade level, and sixth-graders read Shakespeare and Tolstoy. Significantly, Collins emphasizes the classics over today's dull textbooks, and she groups students by academic ability rather than age.[9]

[7]Walter Williams, "Minority Children Need Education Vouchers," *Orange County Register*, May 20, 1993.

[8]"Uncovering the Hidden Treasures in Our Inner City Schools," *Urban Family* (a quarterly journal published by the John M. Perkins Foundation for Reconciliation and Development, Pasadena, Calif.), Fall 1993, p. 22.

[9]Ibid.

The amazing thing isn't that schools like Marcus Garvey and Westside Prep exist, but that most government schools so resolutely ignore their success.

Independent School Performance

Lacking the luxury of compelled attendance and guaranteed tax revenue, independent schools like Marcus Garvey must shape themselves to the desires of the parents and the needs of the children they serve. This has much to do with their superior performance. Parents do not make the financial sacrifice required for independent school tuition unless the school meets their expectations. Those expectations vary, but among the most common are safety, discipline, the teaching of moral values, high expectations, a challenging curriculum, and academic excellence.

Disadvantaged government school students seeking a better education don't need a high-profile alternative like Marcus Garvey or Westside Prep; the local Catholic school will almost always be an improvement. A University of Maryland study shows that merely attending a Catholic rather than a government high school raises the disadvantaged student's probability of completing high school and entering a four-year college by 20 percentage points.[10] "The main source of Catholic schools' success in the classroom is simple," states *U.S. News & World Report.* "They stick to the basics rather than put a lot of money they don't have into fancy equipment, elective courses and extracurricular activities. They push kids to take tough courses like algebra and advanced English. They put a lot of emphasis on foreign languages and very little on vocational education."[11]

Government schoolteachers in some urban areas are twice as likely as the general public to put their own children in independent schools, according to a 1986 study by Denis Doyle and Terry Hartle

[10]Study authors Bill Evans and Robert Schwab review data from 13,294 students in 1,100 schools. "Disadvantaged" students include those with family incomes under $7,000 annually and those whose parents were high school dropouts. See Tamara Henry, "Catholic-School Pupils Take Education Further," *USA Today*, February 22, 1994, p. 4D.

[11]"Parochial Schools: An Evolving Mission," *U.S. News & World Report*, December 9, 1991, pp. 68–71.

of the American Enterprise Institute.[12] If you believe the president of the National Education Association, the proportion is even higher than that. On the August 29, 1993, edition of ABC's "This Week with David Brinkley," journalist George Will asserted that 50 percent of urban government schoolteachers send their children to independent schools. "It's about 40 percent," responded NEA president Keith Geiger.[13] One such teacher explains why:

> Every morning, Gladys Reyes heads off to her job as a kindergarten teacher at Peabody Elementary School in Chicago.
> But she takes her 8-year-old son and 5-year-old daughter to the local Catholic school.
> Why would a public school teacher turn her back on her own school by sending her kids to a private school?
> Religion's one reason, she says. Discipline's another. But she also feels public schools have their problems.
> "I blame the system," she says. . . .
> Whatever the numbers, Gladys Reyes . . . says she's doing what's best for her kids.
> "Every individual person looks out for their own," she says. "I'm looking out for my children's education. And if I don't feel they're getting a good education, I'm going to look someplace else."[14]

American Federation of Teachers president Albert Shanker argues that independent schools do no better than government schools, or that if they do, it is only because they select better students in the first place. As evidence, he claims that government and independent school students have virtually identical math scores on the National Assessment of Educational Progress (NAEP).[15]

Shanker's argument is disingenuous at best. NAEP tests students in the 4th, 8th, and 12th grades. On the 1990 NAEP, the average

[12]The study considered 21 cities in 13 states. Because it relied in part on 1980 Census data, teachers union officials dispute the continuing validity of its conclusions. However, it seems highly unlikely that the number is decreasing. Dennis Kelly, "Teachers Who Go Private—For Own Kids," *USA Today*, October 15, 1993, p. 2D.

[13]Peter Brimelow and Leslie Spencer, "Union Knows Best," *Forbes*, October 11, 1993, p. 89; Kelly, "Teachers Who Go Private," p. 2D.

[14]Kelly, "Teachers Who Go Private," pp. 1D–2D.

[15]Dennis Kelly, "Trying to Quantify the Difference," *USA Today*, February 17, 1993, p. 7D.

4th-grade math scores are 214 for government school students, 224 for Catholic school students, and 231 for other independent school students (on a scale from 0 to 500). By the 12th grade the gap has narrowed, but Catholic and other independent school students still score six to seven points higher.[16] Chubb and Moe point out that scores are closer in the 12th grade because by then the worst government school students have dropped out (about one-fifth of them) and many students who attended independent elementary schools (about one-third of them) have transferred into government high schools.[17] Moreover, independent schools score significantly higher than the government schools on the NAEP writing tests.

Probably the most thorough comparison of government and independent school performance is that of Chubb and Moe. Among their findings: the government school dropout rate is 24 percent; the independent school rate is half that. One-third of government school seniors take the SAT, with an average score of 896; *two*-thirds of independent school students take it, with an average score of 932. Fewer than 30 percent of government high school graduates go directly to four-year colleges; more than 50 percent of independent school graduates do. Six years after high school, only 13 percent of government school graduates have bachelor's degrees (9 percent of blacks and Hispanics), contrasted to 31 percent of independent school grads (25 percent for blacks and Hispanics). Independent schools can select their students, yet most are not very selective; they can expel their students, yet "public schools actually lose or get rid of more problem students." In terms of parental involvement, "private schools get more participation out of parents of lower socioeconomic status than public schools get out of parents of higher socioeconomic status."[18]

Why the differences? Chubb and Moe conclude that they "have a lot to do with the differences between politics and markets—especially with the absence or presence of choice." Government schools report to political authorities through a bureaucratic regime subject to a panoply of interest-group pressures. Independent schools, in contrast, focus exclusively on parental expectations. In defense of the government schools, Chubb and Moe add:

[16]Ibid.

[17]John E. Chubb and Terry M. Moe, "The Private vs. Public School Debate," *Wall Street Journal*, July 26, 1991.

[18]Ibid.

> Public schools could—and would—do things differently if
> they were subject to different pressures. The lesson of public-
> private comparisons is not that private schools are better
> than public schools. It is that market pressures encourage the
> development of better schools than political pressures do.[19]

School choice replaces political pressures with market forces and replaces direct government control of schools with free parental choice. This makes it easier for government schools to emulate the good qualities of independent schools; if they fail to do so, it makes it easier for parents to afford independent schools.

And affordability is the only thing standing between many parents and independent schools. A *Los Angeles Times* Orange County poll released on June 13, 1993, showed that *only 37 percent* of parents with children in government schools would keep them there if California's Parental Choice in Education Initiative passed. Well over half the parents wanted to get their kids out. These are remarkable numbers; Orange County is a relatively prosperous area with generally well-regarded schools, and even there the parents want out. Orange County is not an aberration. According to a 1991 poll by the National Association of Independent Schools (NAIS), *51 percent of parents nationwide* would send their children to independent schools if cost were not a factor.[20]

As of 1990, according to the National Center for Education Statistics, 11 percent of elementary and secondary students were attending independent schools.[21] Some estimates are higher, ranging from 12 percent to 13 percent.[22] For the 1992–93 school year, nationwide independent school enrollment was 5.2 million, compared to government school enrollment of 41.8 million.[23] Catholic school enrollment accounts for about half the independent school total. In California, independent schools now educate well over half a million students,

[19]Ibid.

[20]Tamara Henry, "What's Best for the Children?" *USA Today,* February 17, 1993, p. 7D.

[21]"Slippery Statistics: Where Do Teachers Send Their Kids?" *USA Today,* February 17, 1993, p. 9D.

[22]See, for example, Brimelow and Spencer, p. 89.

[23]Henry, "What's Best for the Children?" p. 7D.

the great majority in church-affiliated schools.[24] Many more parents, the *Times* and NAIS surveys indicate, would choose such schools if they could.

Values

Many parents are dissatisfied not only with government schools' academic offerings, but also with their failure to transmit or even respect basic virtues. Of the *Times* survey respondents who wanted to pull their children out of government schools, more than half wanted to put them into church-affiliated schools. Some parents want their children to receive instruction in religion along with other subjects. Others, while not desiring a specifically religious education, agree that schools should not be value-neutral. Independent schools respond to such parents in a way that the government school system does not.

Supreme Court decisions, appropriately, forbid government schools to impose any religious observance on their students. But most schools have gone further than the Court requires, withdrawing almost entirely from the moral realm. So skittish are they of anything remotely religious that discussions of ethics and values are rare, and coverage of subjects such as the religious influences on American and world history has all but disappeared.

Parents choose church-affiliated schools for many reasons, including physical safety and academic discipline. Clearly, though, moral education is a key consideration. A particular concern for some is the extent to which state-mandated family-life programs have, in the words of New Jersey high school senior E. V. Kontorovich, "drifted from sex education toward sex preparation." Kontorovich describes repeated condom drills in his health class and observes:

> Amid all this hands-on instruction, of course, abstinence, which requires neither a gadget nor training, gets short shrift: It is mentioned once in a video but is not assigned further discussion or study.
>
> My sex-ed experience is far from atypical. According to the Eagleton survey, virtually all high-school health teachers [in New Jersey] and more than half of middle-school health

[24]For the 1987–88 school year, California private schools enrolled 528,561 students. Of that number, 394,909 attended church-affiliated schools. James S. Fay, ed., *California Almanac*, 5th ed. (Santa Barbara: Pacific Data Resources, 1991), p. 64.

teachers instruct students in contraceptive methods. . . . Students across the country are being exposed to contraception kits with mock phalluses and cervixes. . . .

Obviously, this is an extremely mechanistic—and limited—view of sex. In my school, there is little difference in tone between our sex education classes and the defensive driving courses we took in the 10th grade. Both are seen as natural, even ubiquitous, activities that can be made safe with a few pointers.

But focusing on the physical details of sex is value-laden in itself and misleads students. It strips away the ethics that inform human sexuality. Schools should not preach values, but there is a difference between that and pointing out that they exist, and are inseparable from some aspects of life.[25]

Many parents sacrifice to put their children into schools that reaffirm, rather than undercut, what they try to teach at home. School choice would enable many more children to attend such schools. Of course, it would also broaden the opportunities for parents who desired explicitly secular schools for their children. By enabling every parent to afford an independent school, a tuition voucher system would give rise to a much greater variety of independent schools.

Independent School Costs

When most people think of private education, they imagine elite college preparatory academies or distant boarding schools that only the very wealthy can afford. Thus they mistakenly assume that independent schools are quite expensive. In reality, such institutions constitute only a very small percentage of independent schools. The more typical independent school is a modest church-sponsored day school whose cost per pupil is less than half that of government schools in the area.

According to a nationwide study by economist Robert Genetski, "Average cost data for public and private education indicate that in 1990 the operating cost per student for kindergarten through grade 12 in public schools was $4,841, compared with private school costs of $1,902."[26] The U.S. Department of Education reports that

[25]E. V. Kontorovich, "Sex Prep, Not Sex Ed," *Wall Street Journal*, June 21, 1993, p. A10.

[26]Robert Genetski, "Private Schools, Public Savings," *Wall Street Journal*, July 8, 1992.

Catholic schools charge an average annual tuition of $1,327; other church-sponsored independent schools charge an average of $1,941; and nonsectarian independent schools charge an average of $3,839— all far below the per-pupil cost to the taxpayers of the government school system.[27]

The largest single provider of independent schooling is the Catholic school system. Nationwide, its tuition averages about $1,000 for elementary students, $2,500 for high schoolers.[28] How can the Catholic schools perform so well with so little money? Some educrats charge that they are able to do so only because the teachers have taken vows of poverty, but relatively few Catholic school teachers today are members of the religious orders. A more pertinent reason is that the Catholic schools spend their money teaching children instead of maintaining a bureaucracy. For example, the Archdiocese of Washington, D.C., educates 50,000 students with a central administrative staff of 17. The government school system of Washington, D.C., with 81,000 students, has a central administrative staff of 1,500. "Not surprisingly," notes *U.S. News & World Report*, "Catholic schools educate students less expensively than do public schools."[29]

The educrats claim that parochial school tuition figures understate the actual cost per student because the Church subsidizes the schools. It is true that tuition payments cover only about two-thirds of the average Catholic school's cost. The difference is attributable in part to the Church's determination to educate inner-city students and provide the financial aid necessary to do so. The educrats' argument misses the point, though; even with Church support and all other costs factored in, the per-pupil cost of parochial schools remains less than half that of the government schools. The figures from a typical Catholic school system appear in Table 5.1. Catholic students receive a discount, as do additional children from the same family, Catholic or not.[30] Tuition covers only 64 percent of the average per-pupil cost, but the average total cost is still under $2,000.[31]

[27]National Center for Education Statistics, Office of Educational Research and Improvement, U.S. Department of Education, *Digest of Education Statistics 1992* (Washington: NCES 92–097, 1992), p. 71.

[28]"Parochial Schools: An Evolving Mission," p. 71.

[29]Ibid.

[30]Diocese of Fresno Education Corporation, "1991–1992 Tuition Report Card," September 27, 1991, p. 1.

[31]Ibid., p. 3.

Table 5.1
TUITION CHARGED VS. ACTUAL COST PER STUDENT, PAROCHIAL SCHOOLS, DIOCESE OF FRESNO, CALIFORNIA

	Tuition Paid by Non-Catholic Student	Total Cost per Student
Elementary Schools		
Bakersfield	$1,707	$2,260
Fresno	1,567	1,927
Hanford	1,472	1,851
Merced	1,613	1,851
High Schools		
Diocesan average	$3,500	$4,675

SOURCE: Diocese of Fresno Education Corporation, "1991–1992 Tuition Report Card," September 27, 1991, pp. 1–4.

The Sacramento Diocese reports even lower numbers: an average tuition of $1,047 and an annual total cost per pupil of $1,562.[32] The per-pupil cost of California's government school system, in contrast, is over $5,200.[33] Around the country the figures are much the same. The Milwaukee Diocese, for example, has 34,045 elementary students and 7,178 high school students. Average total cost per elementary pupil is $1,694; per high school student, $3,854. Over 22 percent of the students are non-Catholic.[34]

Even in expensive areas, like California's Orange County, tuition at church-sponsored independent schools are low. David Rolph, school superintendent for Calvary Chapel in Costa Mesa, reports that the most expensive tuition any student can pay in his school is $3,000. That's for a high school student who is not a member of the sponsoring church. Average elementary school tuition is $2,000. "We're probably pretty typical," Rolph says.[35] The Association of

[32]Glenn E. Noreen, "Comparison of Public and Private School Financial Statements," presented to Legislative Analyst Office, State of California, June 20, 1993.

[33]Letter from Thomas W. Hayes, director of finance, state of California, to state senator Bill Leonard, dated September 24, 1991; see Chapter 3.

[34]John J. Stollenwerk, letter, *Business Week*, October 26, 1992, p. 10.

[35]Interview with Bob and Geri Boyd, of Costa Mesa, California, on "Parents, It's Your Choice," the April 25, 1992, edition of "Issues in Education," a syndicated radio program. Tape in possession of author.

Christian Schools International reports that "almost all" of its 750 member schools in California charge less than $2,500 per year.[36] Other church-affiliated schools have similarly low costs. Nationwide, 95 percent of Catholic schools and 88 percent of Protestant schools charge annual tuition of $2,500 or less.[37]

Independent School Students

The lower cost and higher performance of independent schools is all the more impressive in light of their diverse student body. Nationally, minority enrollment constitutes 23 percent of the Catholic school population, and the rates of graduation and college attendance for minority students in Catholic schools surpass those of their peers in government schools significantly.[38] Minority children generally receive the same attention and encouragement as the others, and they are placed in the same rigorous academic tracks. Other church-sponsored schools are also educating growing numbers of minority students, many of whom are not members of the sponsoring church.

In California, nearly half of all independent school students attend Catholic schools; and more than half of Catholic school students are blacks, Hispanics, Asians, and Native Americans. The so-called minorities are a majority. (See Table 5.2.)

Many independent schools focus specifically on the needs of children with physical or mental handicaps.[39] These schools demonstrate an important fact: what makes independent schools unique is not the nature of their student body, but the way in which the student body is treated. The strong record of independent schools cannot be dismissed as the result of selective admissions. It's not who enters the school, but what happens to them while they're there, that makes the difference.

[36]"Stop Lying!" Fact sheet issued by ACSI in 1992 rebutting California Teachers Assocation claims of high private school tuition.

[37]Department of Commerce, *1991 Statistical Abstract of the United States* (Washington: Government Printing Office, 1991); calculation made from reported private school tuitions.

[38]"Parochial Schools: An Evolving Mission," pp. 68–71.

[39]Special education is not limited to the government school system. In California many government schools refer children with special needs to the California Association of Private Special Education Schools. CAPSES members give personalized help to students facing a daunting variety of physical and mental challenges.

Table 5.2
PERCENTAGE OF MINORITY STUDENTS
ATTENDING CALIFORNIA PAROCHIAL ELEMENTARY SCHOOLS

Diocese	Total Students	Percentage Minority
Los Angeles	70,192	68.3
Oakland	15,379	55.8
San Francisco	20,943	53.8
San Bernardino	8,242	48.4
San Diego	12,412	44.4
Orange	12,842	39.8
San Jose	9,245	39.4
Sacramento	13,022	37.1
Stockton	3,343	36.3
Fresno	5,795	32.9
Monterey	3,596	25.8
Santa Rosa	2,999	15.4
Total	178,010	53.6

SOURCE: "California Catholic Schools Report," Enrollment 1991–92, California Catholic Conference, Division of Education, November 27, 1991.

Independent schools teach differently. Few of their teachers have degrees in education; most have degrees in the subjects they teach. Salaries are somewhat lower than in the government school system, yet independent schools appear to have no trouble attracting qualified teachers. Perhaps teachers who choose independent schools find that favorable working conditions and a high degree of autonomy are important elements of their compensation.[40]

Speaking of compensation, some teachers work for no pay at all—in home schools. Estimates of the number vary from 300,000 to 1 million. Whatever the number, it appears to be growing. Once perceived as the province of religious fundamentalists, home schooling is now moving into the mainstream, attracting parents of every religious persuasion, including no religious persuasion. Dissatisfaction with the government schools is their common motivation; they want a stronger academic foundation for their children.

[40]"The Flight from Public Schools," U.S. News & World Report, December 9, 1991, pp. 72–73.

Home-taught children overall match or beat their school-taught peers on standardized tests and appear to adapt just as well socially.[41]

What Makes Them Work?

The educrats plainly do not like all this independent schooling. They tolerate it as long as they have an exclusive on the tax dollars, but any school choice plan in which the dollar follows the scholar to a school they don't run is absolute anathema. They are particularly bothered by the prospect of for-profit schools. "Skeptics are questioning the effects of profiting on an enterprise like education," reports *U.S. News*. "They worry first about the temptation of school owners with their eyes on the bottom line to cut corners, compromising academic quality in the process."[42]

As if the government schools were guardians of academic quality! Please. The alternative to the profit motive is the loss motive. We've seen how well *that* works.

The effective schools research of the last two decades, not to mention countless reform commissions, rediscovered the obvious. Successful schools—those that do a good job of preparing their students for productive work, for higher education, and for responsible citizenship—tend to have clear missions, rigorous standards, consistent discipline, challenging coursework and homework, autonomy for teachers, teachers professional enough to use their autonomy productively, strong leaders for their principals, and high expectations of everybody. Until Chubb and Moe, however, nobody carefully researched how these characteristics developed, so the reformers just mandated that schools display them. Those very mandates became part of the problem. Leadership, high expectations, a sense of mission, and the other characteristics of effective schools are not amenable to legislation. They are individual and internal. They need freedom and competition to emerge and thrive.

But freedom and competition are antithetical to the government school system, a classically socialist enterprise owned and operated

---

[41]"Teaching Children at Home," *Bottom Line/Personal*, July 15, 1993, p. 8, reviewing study led by J. Gary Knowles, University of Michigan at Ann Arbor; Kristin Davis and Kim Quillen, "The Economics of Teaching Your Kids at Home," *Kiplinger's Personal Finance Magazine*, July 1993, p. 30; "Capitol Flood," editorial, *Wall Street Journal*, March 2, 1994, p. A14; and Steve Stecklow, "Fed Up with Schools, More Parents Turn to Teaching at Home," *Wall Street Journal*, May 10, 1994, p. A1.

[42]"The Flight from Public Schools," p. 77.

by the state, administered through a cumbersome bureaucracy, subject to a panoply of political pressures, and insulated from the individual desires manifested by the market. It is a near monopoly, its 90 percent market share all but guaranteed. It faces no real competition: very few parents are able to choose alternatives, and even if they do the system's funding is usually unaffected.

Since the government schools have a captive market, they don't need to improve to keep their customers; most customers have nowhere else to go. Occasionally a great success story emerges from somewhere in the system or from the independent schools—and most government schools keep right on doing what they were already doing. Success is barely observed, when in a free market it would be assiduously imitated.

The independent schools are a different story: no captive clientele for them. Either they please the customer and justify that tuition bill by providing a good education, or the customer walks. And a remarkable thing happens. Without any legislators telling them to do so and without any bureaucrats supervising, the independent schools do an outstanding job. Each school decides on its own what to teach, who will teach it, and how to go about the whole process. Parents make their own choices based on what they know will work best for their own children. Nobody imposes decisions on anyone; everyone makes decisions for themselves.

And the children thrive. In the best schools they not only achieve more academically, they are happier. They don't need to fear going to the bathroom or the wrong area of the playground. They are not just a number to the school's administrators. They are not just doing time. They are intellectually and socially alive. They are challenged, encouraged, helped, and loved.

Some schools, both government and independent, provide such an environment; most schools do not. Why should parents be forced to keep their children in any school that does not meet their needs? Where another school can do a better job for less money, why not enable the child to attend that school instead?

That is the goal of school choice.

PART II

THE CALIFORNIA CAMPAIGN

6. The Parental Choice in Education Initiative: Text and Analysis

Most school districts make enrollment assignments without regard to student or parent preference. Students are typically assigned to the school nearest their home. Occasionally, they are assigned elsewhere for administrative reasons such as racial balance. But the administrators who determine enrollment generally do not even consider the unique aptitudes and interests of individual students and the learning environment that would best foster their growth. School choice changes that. It offers other options, allowing parents to determine which available schools best meet the needs of their children.

The term "school choice" is used to describe three separate kinds of programs. The first and narrowest is intradistrict choice—permitting parents or students to choose any school within a given government school district. This is certainly better than restricting enrollment to a particular school; some choice is better than none. However, limiting the choice to government schools in a given district is like saying you can buy any car as long as it's a Buick. Being allowed to choose from among a Roadmaster, Park Avenue, or LeSabre doesn't feel like much of a choice if what you had in mind was a Honda or Toyota. Intradistrict choice is a step in the right direction, but it leaves more options closed than open.

The second kind of program is interdistrict choice, or open enrollment—permitting enrollment at any government school in the state. This is a further step in the right direction, but again it stops short of full choice. It's like saying you can buy any car as long as it's built by General Motors; while that allows a choice of several makes and models, it isn't much of a choice if your preferred car comes from a competing manufacturer.

The third and most comprehensive kind of school choice, sometimes called a voucher system, allows a student to choose among not only government schools but independent schools as well. The choice is financed through a state-issued voucher worth up to a specified dollar amount that can be redeemed at participating schools for tuition. In this book, the term "school choice" refers to that kind of plan. For an excellent overview of the three kinds of school choice and examples of each, see Edward B. Fiske, *Smart Schools, Smart Kids* (New York: Simon & Schuster, 1991) pp. 164–202.

The conceptual roots of school choice go back more than two centuries to the great economist Adam Smith, but the first explicit proposal to implement school choice through tuition vouchers came from Nobel laureate Milton Friedman. Friedman has been the leading advocate of school choice for a generation.[1] In recent years he has seen several parental choice proposals introduced as legislation or placed on state ballots as citizen initiatives. The most prominent of these has been California's Proposition 174, the Parental Choice in Education Initiative. Friedman publicly endorsed Proposition 174, calling it "by far the best formulated version that has yet been put to the voters anywhere."[2] Not surprisingly, Proposition 174 is serving as a model for school choice proposals in other states.

Proposition 174 focused renewed attention on the persistently poor performance of the government school system and the growing demand for alternatives to it. The education establishment managed to defeat the initiative only by spending over $14 million on a highly misleading negative campaign. The best way to understand the initiative, and to dismiss the accusations against it, is to read it. Accordingly the full text of the initiative is reproduced below, with explanatory comments. (The text is distinguished by boldface type.)

The Parental Choice in Education Initiative

The following Section, the "Parental Choice in Education Amendment," is hereby added to Article IX of the California Constitution:

COMMENT: It was both legally and politically necessary to draft this school choice proposal as an initiative amending the state constitution. The legal necessity arises because much of the law governing elementary and secondary education in California is constitutional rather

---

[1]See Milton Friedman, *Capitalism and Freedom* (Chicago: University of Chicago Press, 1962); and Milton Friedman and Rose D. Friedman, *Free to Choose* (New York: Harcourt Brace Jovanovich, 1980), pp. 158–75.

[2]Milton Friedman, "Dear Interested Citizen," letter, August 19, 1993, p. 2; copy in possession of author.

than merely statutory. The California Constitution obligates the state to maintain a system of common schools, mandates minimum funding levels, and prohibits state funding of church-sponsored schools. School choice requires flexibility that these provisions prohibit unless amended.

The political necessity arises because the education committees in the state senate and assembly are unremittingly hostile to school choice. As documented in Chapter 4, the California Teachers Association spends more than any other organization on lobbying state legislators, and it contributes heavily to the campaigns of its allies on the education committees. No meaningful choice legislation will emerge from either committee without a dramatic change in membership. Moreover, were the initiative merely statutory, it would be eviscerated by the legislature. Thus it was necessary to take a constitutional amendment directly to the people.

Section 17. Purpose. The people of California, desiring to improve the quality of education available to all children, adopt this Section to: (1) enable parents to determine which schools best meet their children's needs; (2) empower parents to send their children to such schools; (3) establish academic accountability based on national standards; (4) reduce bureaucracy so that more educational dollars reach the classroom; (5) provide greater opportunities for teachers; and (6) mobilize the private sector to help accommodate our burgeoning school-age population.

COMMENT: This supplicating language has no direct legal effect, but it explains the motivations of initiative proponents and the objectives of school choice.

Therefore: All parents are hereby empowered to choose any school, public or private, for the education of their children, as provided in this Section.

(a) Empowerment of Parents; Granting of Scholarships. The State shall annually provide a scholarship to every resident school-age child. Scholarships may be redeemed by the child's parent at any scholarship-redeeming school.

(1) The scholarship value for each child shall be at least fifty percent of the average amount of State and local government spending per public school student for education in kindergarten and

grades one through twelve during the preceding fiscal year, calculated on a statewide basis, including every cost to the State, school districts, and county offices of education of maintaining kindergarten and elementary and secondary education, but excluding expenditures on scholarships granted pursuant to this Section and excluding any unfunded pension liability associated with the public school system.

COMMENT: The initiative authorizes parents to select whatever school, government or independent, that best meets the needs of their children. If parents choose a government school, the regular amount of public funding follows their child to that school. If parents choose an independent school instead, they may obtain a state-funded scholarship, or tuition voucher, worth at least half the per-pupil cost of the government schools. For the fiscal year in which the initiative was submitted (1991–92), that cost was $5,242; thus the minimum scholarship amount that year would have been $2,621.

Note that the funding formula is definite enough to guarantee the program's continuation, yet simple and flexible enough to work as a permanent part of the state constitution. The drafters avoided the rigid extreme of specifying dollar amounts because inflation, fiscal policy, and other factors would inevitably alter the dollar amounts necessary and available. The drafters also avoided the opposite extreme of leaving the scholarship amount entirely to legislative discretion because of the obvious political danger to school choice from the education establishment. The initiative takes a middle course: the scholarship value will be at least half of whatever it costs the government to run its own schools.

In essence, the initiative tells parents dissatisfied with the government schools, "If you can find a better education for half the price, please take advantage of it! You'll save the state money." More importantly, of course, free choice among competing schools promises to improve the quality of education available to all children.

As Chapter 5 shows, the cost of attending the average independent school is substantially *less* than the minimum scholarship amount. Thus, the initiative makes independent school a realistic option for all families, regardless of income.

(2) Scholarship value shall be equal for every child in any given grade. In case of student transfer, the scholarship shall be prorated.

The Legislature may award supplemental funds for reasonable transportation needs for low-income children and special needs attributable to physical impairment or learning disability. Nothing in this Section shall prevent the use in any school of supplemental assistance from any source, public or private.

COMMENT: Generally, higher grade levels have higher costs; thus the initiative allows (but does not require) the scholarship value to vary from one grade to another. For example, the legislature might decide to increase the scholarship amount for high school students. But no scholarship for any grade level can fall below the minimum value of approximately $2,621.

The initiative's goal is not to ship low-income students to distant schools but to enable good schools to flourish in their own neighborhoods. Chapter 5 notes that good schools already exist in many places, even in the inner cities. The barrier isn't transportation, but tuition. Thus the initiative makes transportation funding optional and scholarship funding mandatory.

Many independent special education schools already exist. Naturally, their costs tend to exceed the average. This provision invites the legislature to extend the scholarship program to students with special needs so they can choose such schools. Since many government programs affect services to special education students, it would be unwise to permanently mandate a particular program in a constitutional amendment. Thus the initiative authorizes supplemental expenditures rather than requiring them.

(3) If the scholarship amount exceeds the charges imposed by a scholarship-redeeming school for any year in which the student is in attendance, the surplus shall become a credit held in trust by the State for the student for later application toward charges at any scholarship-redeeming school or any institution of higher education in California, public or private, which meets the requirements imposed on scholarship-redeeming schools in Section 17(b)(1) and (3). Any surplus remaining on the student's twenty-sixth birthday shall revert to the State treasury.

COMMENT: If an independent school charges more than the scholarship amount, the parents are responsible for the difference. If it charges less, the difference is held in trust for the child's future education. Without this provision, the scholarships could have an inflationary impact; every school would want to charge at least the full scholarship amount. This provision gives schools an incentive to restrain their costs by giving parents an incentive to choose lower-cost schools. It also offers students a new source of college scholarship money at no new cost to the state.

(4) Scholarships provided hereunder are grants of aid to children through their parents and not to the schools in which the children are enrolled. Such scholarships shall not constitute taxable income. The parent shall be free to choose any scholarship-redeeming school, and such selection shall not constitute a decision or act of the State or any of its subdivisions. No other provision of this Constitution shall prevent the implementation of this Section.

COMMENT: This paragraph enables church-sponsored schools to participate in the school choice program without running afoul of what is commonly called the doctrine of separation of church and state. Parents may use tuition vouchers at any qualifying school, including a church-sponsored school. The choice of school is a parental decision, not a state directive. This does not constitute state funding of religion any more than food stamps constitute state funding of supermarkets.

The last sentence of this paragraph overrides, rather than explicitly repeals, potentially conflicting portions of the state constitution. This sentence is narrowly tailored to allow implementation of the initiative with the minimum possible disruption of existing law.

(5) Children enrolled in private schools on October 1, 1991, shall receive scholarships, if otherwise eligible, beginning with the 1995–96 fiscal year. All other children shall receive scholarships beginning with the 1993–94 fiscal year.

COMMENT: Government school students who use scholarships to transfer to independent schools will save the state money. However, existing independent school students who take scholarships will cost the state money. This provision gives government school students access to the scholarships two years before independent school students, thus allowing the state to accumulate a pool of savings from which to fund the later inclusion of independent school students. This provision is intended to ensure that the initiative imposes no net costs on the taxpayers.

(Note: Proponents expected the initiative to be on the 1992 ballot and intended it to take effect in the following fiscal year. Because it appeared on the 1993 ballot instead, under California legal precedent the effective dates would have been adjusted accordingly.)

(6) The State Board of Education may require each public school and each scholarship-redeeming school to choose and administer tests reflecting national standards for the purpose of measuring individual academic improvement. Such tests shall be designed and scored by independent parties. Each school's composite results for each grade level shall be released to the public. Individual results shall be released only to the school and the child's parent.

COMMENT: Since students vary widely in background and ability, some schools have a tougher job than others. Thus perhaps the fairest way to assess school performance is through tests measuring individual academic "improvement" as well as "achievement." If the state requires such tests, it must require them of government and scholarship-redeeming schools alike and must make results public. This should help parents determine which school best suits their children.

The state may require that testing occur, but it cannot mandate the use of any particular test; schools choose which tests to use. Moreover, the state is not authorized to require testing of anything beyond individual academic improvement. This protects independent schools against state encroachment. It also fosters diversity, competition, and improvement in the field of testing.

(7) Governing boards of school districts shall establish a mechanism consistent with federal law to allocate enrollment capacity based primarily on parental choice. Any public school which chooses not to redeem scholarships shall, after district enrollment assignments based primarily on parental choice are complete, open its remaining enrollment capacity to children regardless of residence. For fiscal purposes, children shall be deemed residents of the school district in which they are enrolled.

COMMENT: Except for those under court desegregation orders, government school districts generally assign children to particular schools on the basis of geography: you attend the school within whose boundaries you reside. Parental preference is not considered. Parents dissatisfied with the assigned school may request intra- or interdistrict transfers, but these may be denied at the district's discretion.

Under the initiative parental preference is the first, rather than the last, consideration. District administrators must determine which schools parents want their children to attend. Some districts that allow choice within their own system already do this by having parents indicate their first, second, and third choices on a ballot. Many students are able to attend their first choice, and most are able to attend one of their top three.

After parents living within the district have made their choices, any remaining capacity must be opened to children from outside the district. This reduces the need for new school construction by using existing facilities more optimally. It also makes administrators more clearly aware of which schools satisfy parents and which do not. As with other provisions of the initiative, this saves tax money and spurs educational improvement simultaneously.

For government schools and independent schools alike, the dollar follows the scholar. Districts attracting more students receive more money; districts from which students flee receive less. That should focus their attention.

(8) No child shall receive any scholarship under this Section or any credit under Section 17(a)(3) for any fiscal year in which the child enrolls in a non-scholarship-redeeming school, unless the Legislature provides otherwise.

COMMENT: Once a student enrolls in any school that does not accept scholarships, his or her choice for that year is made; he or she cannot receive a scholarship until the following year. This provision deters frivolous transfers.

(b) Empowerment of Schools; Redemption of Scholarships. A private school may become a scholarship-redeeming school by filing with the State Board of Education a statement indicating satisfaction of the legal requirements which applied to private schools on October 1, 1991, and the requirements of this Section.

COMMENT: The key precondition for the continued success of independent schools is their relative freedom from state control.

The initiative safeguards that freedom by preventing the imposition of new laws and regulations as a condition of redeeming scholarships. Any school complying with the laws and regulations governing independent schools as of October 1, 1991, and complying with the additional requirements of the initiative itself, may redeem scholarships. The drafters selected a date preceding the official submission of the initiative to ensure that the school choice program would not be thwarted by subsequent legislation.

Numerous state laws already govern independent schools and will continue to do so under the initiative. These laws deal with course requirements for graduation; teacher qualifications; health and safety regulations; earthquake safety; and employee behavior.[3]

(1) No school which discriminates on the basis of race, ethnicity, color, or national origin may redeem scholarships.

COMMENT: This could not be clearer. If a school excludes a student because of race, the Parental Choice in Education Initiative excludes that school.

Gender is not listed because some parents—and a growing number of educators and researchers—believe that students are better able to focus on learning in a single-sex environment.[4] Some highly respected colleges, like Wellesley, operate on the same premise.

Religion is not listed because many parents seeking alternatives to the government schools—a majority of them, in some surveys—want their children to be able to attend church-sponsored schools. While most church sponsored schools welcome students of any (or no) religious persuasion, some have good reasons for favoring

---

[3]California Education Code, sections 48222, 51202, 51210, 51220, and 51225.3; California Education Code, section 48222; California Health and Safety Code, sections 1500 to 1565 and section 3381 (see also regulations of the state fire marshal and the State Department of Health Services; in addition, numerous city and county agencies impose health and safety standards on private schools); California Education Code, sections 35296 to 35298; California Education Code, section 44237; and California Penal Code, section 11166.

[4]For a review of the "growing evidence that girls do better without boys" in class, see Sharon Massey, "Co-Ed Schools Are Studying All-Girl Classes," *Wall Street Journal*, September 10, 1993, p. B1. For an explanation of the usefulness of all-male classes, particularly in predominantly black schools, see "Uncovering the Hidden Treasures in Our Inner City Schools," *Urban Family* (a quarterly journal published by the John M. Perkins Foundation for Reconciliation and Development, Pasadena, Calif.), Fall 1993, p. 23.

members of their own denomination or congregation. Moreover, many of them consider a code of conduct incorporating religious values an essential component of their mission. Further, as a practical matter, the majority of existing private schools are church-sponsored. Excluding them would severely constrain, rather than expand, parental choices and educational opportunities.

Disability is not listed because discrimination on that basis is already forbidden by broader federal and state law. No school, government or independent, accommodates every kind of disability. Among both government and independent schools one finds specialized schools geared toward meeting the needs of students with particular disabilities. Requiring every school to meet the needs of every student is impossible. Paragraph (a)(2) of the initiative encourages expanding the choices of special education students as well as others.

(2) To the extent permitted by this Constitution and the Constitution of the United States, the State shall prevent from redeeming scholarships any school which advocates unlawful behavior; teaches hatred of any person or group on the basis of race, ethnicity, color, national origin, religion, or gender; or deliberately provides false or misleading information respecting the school.

COMMENT: This builds upon the preceding paragraph and speaks for itself. While schools may consider gender and religion for benign purposes—for example, in determining admissions to a Catholic girls school—they may not practice invidious discrimination or teach hatred. The opening phrase automatically adapts the paragraph to developments in First Amendment jurisprudence and state constitutional law.

(3) No school with fewer than 25 students may redeem scholarships, unless the Legislature provides otherwise.

COMMENT: This is one of several antifraud provisions in the initiative. If schools of any size could receive scholarship money, unscrupulous parents might be tempted to establish a small home school and use the money for purposes other than education. Requiring at least 25 students per school is a significant check.

(4) Private schools, regardless of size, shall be accorded maximum flexibility to educate their students and shall be free from unnecessary, burdensome, or onerous regulation. No regulation of private schools, scholarship-redeeming or not, beyond that required by this Section and that which applied to private schools on October 1, 1991, shall be issued or enacted, unless approved by a three-fourths vote of the Legislature or, alternatively, as to any regulation pertaining to health, safety, or land use imposed by any county, city, district, or other subdivision of the State, a two-thirds vote of the governmental body issuing or enacting the regulation and a majority vote of qualified electors within the affected jurisdiction. In any legal proceeding challenging such a regulation as inconsistent with this Section, the governmental body issuing or enacting it shall have the burden of establishing that the regulation: (A) is essential to assure the health, safety, or education of students, or, as to any land use regulation, that the governmental body has a compelling interest in issuing or enacting it; (B) does not unduly burden or impede private schools or the parents of students therein; and (C) will not harass, injure, or suppress private schools.

COMMENT: At present, a simple majority of the state legislature or other governing body can impose new regulation on independent schools. The initiative makes imposing new regulation on *any* independent school, scholarship-redeeming or not, much more difficult. New state regulation can be imposed only by a three-fourths vote in both houses of the state legislature, a very high hurdle. (Most current legislative supermajority requirements specify a two-thirds vote.) New regulation from local entities will require not only a two-thirds vote of the governing body but also approval of a majority of registered voters in the jurisdiction. This prevents such entities from scheduling little-publicized, low-turnout special elections to sneak in new regulation, effectively requiring them to seek voter approval on general election ballots instead.[5]

[5]If this requirement is successfully challenged in court, paragraph (b)(4) softens it without eliminating it. A court might hold that requiring the approval of a majority of all registered voters, whether they actually vote or not, is unconstitutional. The initiative anticipates that possibility and automatically replaces the original requirement with the strictest constitutionally permissible standard. Again, the purpose is to give the maximum possible protection to independent schools.

(5) Notwithstanding Section 17(b)(4), the Legislature may (A) enact civil and criminal penalties for schools and persons who engage in fraudulent conduct in connection with the solicitation of students or the redemption of scholarships, and (B) restrict or prohibit individuals convicted of (i) any felony, (ii) any offense involving lewd or lascivious conduct, or (iii) any offense involving molestation or other abuse of a child, from owning, contracting with, or being employed by any school, public or private.

COMMENT: This is yet another antifraud provision. The initiative protects students, parents, and taxpayers by specifically authorizing the legislature to impose both civil and criminal penalties for fraud. It also authorizes the legislature to require both government and independent schools to take precautions against the employment of unsuitable personnel. Independent school employees are already required by law to submit fingerprints and undergo a criminal clearance investigation.[6] It is hoped that the state will strengthen these requirements and extend them to the government schools for the safety of all children.

The supermajority requirements of paragraph (b)(4) apply only to new laws and regulations going beyond those required by the initiative. They do not apply to antifraud and child protection legislation enacted pursuant to this subsection.

(6) Any school, public or private, may establish a code of conduct and discipline and enforce it with sanctions, including dismissal. A student who is deriving no substantial academic benefit or is responsible for serious or habitual misconduct related to the school may be dismissed.

COMMENT: Again, government and independent schools are placed on a level playing field. While all schools at least theoretically have the authority to expel incorrigible students, some are reluctant to use it, in part because they fear legal challenges. This provision makes their authority clear and prevents the courts from requiring any school to keep troublemakers. The state may need to provide for the education of such students—but not in a conventional school. This paragraph also makes clear the authority of both government and private schools to establish and enforce codes of conduct.

[6]California Education Code, section 44237.

(7) After the parent designates the enrolling school, the State shall disburse the student's scholarship funds, excepting funds held in trust pursuant to Section 17(a)(3), in equal amounts monthly, directly to the school for credit to the parent's account. Monthly disbursals shall occur within 30 days of receipt of the school's statement of current enrollment.

COMMENT: This is yet another antifraud provision, with a new twist; it prevents fraud *by* the state as well as fraud *against* the state. To deter fraud against the state, no school may obtain the entire scholarship amount up front; rather, the scholarships are disbursed in equal amounts monthly. This discourages the establishment of fraudulent schools. Also, no parent receives cash or a cash equivalent; the scholarship funds go directly to the school. This makes parental fraud very difficult.

To deter fraud by the state, the state is required to disburse the monthly scholarship funds to participating schools within 30 days of receiving the school's enrollment list. This prevents the state from delaying payments to qualifying independent schools. Without such protection, the schools would be vulnerable to political games. Delayed payments could seriously interfere with their operations. This provision ensures that independent schools will be compensated reliably for their services.

(8) Expenditures for scholarships issued under this Section and savings resulting from the implementation of this Section shall count toward the minimum funding requirements for education established by Sections 8 and 8.5 of Article XVI. Students enrolled in scholarship-redeeming schools shall not be counted toward enrollment in public schools and community colleges for purposes of Sections 8 and 8.5 of Article XVI.

COMMENT: This provision safeguards the taxpayers. Without it, current state law would require them to pay twice for educating some children. Specifically, Proposition 98 would require funding the government school system as though scholarship-redeeming students were still attending it, even though they had opted for independent schools instead.

Proposition 98 added sections 8 and 8.5 of article XVI to the California Constitution. These sections establish minimum funding requirements for the government school system (including the community college system, but not the state universities). Section 8(b) of article XVI requires the state to spend on the government school system each school year the greater of (Test 1) the amount that equals the percentage of the general fund spent on the government school system in 1986–87 (approximately 42 percent of the general fund) or (Test 2) an amount matching or exceeding the prior year's spending, adjusted for enrollment growth and inflation. A complicated formula (Test 3) requires even greater spending growth in prosperous years. In addition to these expenditures, section 8.5 of article XVI requires the allocation of certain surplus funds to the government school system.

Paragraph (b)(8) of the Parental Choice in Education Initiative partially overrides Proposition 98. The initiative simply says that government schools receive funding only for students actually attending them.

(c) Empowerment of Teachers; Conversion of Schools. Within one year after the people adopt this Section, the Legislature shall establish an expeditious process by which public schools may become independent scholarship-redeeming schools. Such schools shall be common schools under this Article, and Section 6 of this Article shall not limit their formation.

COMMENT: California's existing charter school program allows selected schools to define their own missions and relieves them of much of their regulatory burden. Unfortunately, the program is limited to only 100 schools statewide. Subsection (c) removes that limit, allowing any government school to become a charter school. The initiative does not mandate a particular process, leaving that to be determined by the legislature in accord with changing conditions and increased understanding of what works best.

(1) Except as otherwise required by this Constitution and the Constitution of the United States, such schools shall operate under laws and regulations no more restrictive than those applicable to private schools under Section 17(b).

COMMENT: Government school administrators, who work under a heavy regulatory burden, complain that school choice is unfair to them because it makes them compete with more lightly regulated independent schools. This is a legitimate concern. Paragraph (c)(1) responds to it by offering a way to escape much of the regulatory burden. Government schools may become quasi-independent schools and operate under a regulatory regime no more restrictive than that governing their independent competitors.

Some educrats would prefer to hamstring the independent schools with increased regulation instead. It is an odd approach: since there's a stone in my shoe, let's make the race fair by putting one in yours, too. Why not just remove the stone? The initiative takes the latter approach.

Wherever possible, the initiative imposes the same requirements on, and offers the same opportunities to, government and independent schools alike. (See paragraphs (a)(6), (b)(5), (b)(6), and (c)(1).) Of course, government schools continue to enjoy a significant funding advantage since the base scholarship value is only half the per-pupil cost of government schools. If a student chooses a government school over an independent school, the state will spend twice as much on his or her education.

(2) Employees of such schools shall be permitted to continue and transfer their pension and health care programs on the same terms as other similarly situated participants employed by their school district so long as they remain in the employ of any such school.

COMMENT: This protects the reasonable expectations of teachers and other school employees. This clause does not prevent personnel changes; it simply requires the affected school districts to continue honoring existing commitments to retained personnel. Good teachers have nothing to fear from school choice.

(d) Definitions.

(1) "Charges" include tuition and fees for books, supplies, and other educational costs.

(2) A "child" is an individual eligible to attend kindergarten or grades one through twelve in the public school system.

(3) A "parent" is any person having legal or effective custody of a child.

(4) "Qualified electors" are persons registered to vote, whether or not they vote in any particular election. The alternative requirement in Section 17(b)(4) of approval by a majority vote of qualified electors within the affected jurisdiction shall be imposed

only to the extent permitted by this Constitution and the Constitution of the United States of America.

(5) The Legislature may establish reasonable standards for determining the "residency" of children.

(6) "Savings resulting from the implementation of this Section" in each fiscal year shall be the total amount disbursed for scholarships during that fiscal year subtracted from the product of (A) the average enrollment in scholarship-redeeming schools during that fiscal year multiplied by (B) the average amount of State and local government spending per public school student for education in kindergarten and grades one through twelve, calculated on a statewide basis, during that fiscal year.

(7) A "scholarship-redeeming school" is any school, public or private, located within California, which meets the requirements of this Section. No school shall be compelled to become a scholarship-redeeming school. No school which meets the requirements of this Section shall be prevented from becoming a scholarship-redeeming school.

COMMENT: This definition reemphasizes earlier provisions protecting the autonomy of independent schools. If a school does not wish to accept tuition vouchers, the state cannot force it to. On the other hand, if a school complies with the provisions of the initiative and does wish to accept tuition vouchers, the state cannot prevent it from doing so.

(8) "State and local government spending" in Section 17(a)(1) includes, but is not limited to, spending funded from all revenue sources, including the General Fund, federal funds, local property taxes, lottery funds, and local miscellaneous income such as developer fees, but excludng bond proceeds and charitable donations. Notwithstanding the inclusion of federal funds in the calculation of "state and local government spending," federal funds shall constitute no part of any scholarship provided under this Section.

COMMENT: Excluding federal funding also excludes a host of potential legal and regulatory problems. The scholarships are funded exclusively by the state of California.

(9) A "student" is a child attending school.

(e) Implementation. The legislature shall implement this Section through legislation consistent with the purposes and provisions of this Section.

COMMENT: The initiative does not specify every detail of its implementation and operation, for good reason. The initiative becomes part of the state constitution, which is difficult to amend. Thus it sets forth the policies and purposes of the scholarship program, along with a few essential operational provisions. Details of implementation and administration are left to the legislature, which can modify them as conditions require.

(f) Limitation of actions. Any action or proceeding contesting the validity of (1) this Section, (2) any provision of this Section, or (3) the adoption of this Section, shall be commenced within six months from the date of the election at which this Section is approved; otherwise this Section and all of its provisions shall be held valid, legal, and uncontestable. However, this limitation shall not of itself preclude an action or proceeding to challenge the application of this Section or any of its provisions to a particular person or circumstance.

COMMENT: Interminable legal proceedings could thwart school choice as surely as defeat at the polls. This provision minimizes the possibility of delay in implementation by requiring any legal action challenging the validity of the initiative to be brought within six months of the election.

(g) Severability. If any provision of this Section or the application thereof to any person or circumstance is held invalid, the remaining provisions or applications shall remain in force. To this end the provisions of this Section are severable.

COMMENT: If the courts invalidate any portion of the initiative, the remainder is unaffected.

* * *

In summary, the Parental Choice in Education Initiative makes parental preference the most important factor in school enrollment. Parents within a given school district first choose the schools they prefer. If space remains after district residents have made their choices, it is made available to parents outside the district. State funding follows each child to the enrolling school. No school or district, government or independent, can retain a child if the parents find a preferable alternative elsewhere.

Parents dissatisfied with available government schools may enroll their children in an independent school instead. Such children may receive scholarships worth at least half the preceding fiscal year's per-pupil cost of government education. No parent or school is required to use or accept scholarships, but no qualifying school may be prevented from accepting scholarships. Initial scholarship value would have been about $2,600 per year, an amount that exceeds the average cost of attending independent school both in California and nationwide.

The initiative does not mandate any change in government school funding levels; it merely adjusts the formulas defining existing funding floors to reflect the inclusion of scholarship students. Government school funding beyond the floors remains within the discretion of the legislature, as at present. Children of parents who do not exercise any choice will be automatically assigned to district schools, as at present.

The Parental Choice in Education Initiative restores parents to their rightful role. It gives all parents consumer power in education. It unleashes the greatest force in the world—the love of parents for their children—to determine which schools are working best and to get children into those schools. It unleashes another strong force—competition—by funding schools only to the extent that they attract students. The initiative promises to dramatically improve the quality of education available to the children of any state that adopts it.

7. Objections and Answers

The campaign against Proposition 174 was funded principally by the California Teachers Association (CTA), with help from other government school employee unions and associations.[1] Shortly after the initiative was submitted to the state attorney general for title and summary, the CTA's official newsletter urged its members to defeat the initiative, voicing three concerns:

1. Teacher salaries, benefits, and working conditions might not be secure.
2. Teachers might lose their jobs.
3. Teachers might become subject to the same competitive pressures affecting employees in private enterprise.[2]

The CTA newsletter made no mention whatsoever of quality education for children; the *only* concern was job security.

During the campaign, of course, the CTA and its allies claimed to be motivated by other concerns. Their campaign organization, the Committee to Educate Against Vouchers (CEAV), selected "No on 174, A Risk We Can't Afford" as its motto. The slogan makes little sense, given the academic superiority and cost advantage of independent schools; nevertheless, it proved effective. "A Risk We Can't Afford" served as the umbrella for several attacks against the Parental Choice in Education Initiative:

1. It doesn't regulate the schools it gives money to.
2. It subsidizes the rich.
3. It hurts low-income students.
4. It hurts special education students.

[1] "CTA members financed 80 percent of the campaign's cost by taxing themselves $57 over three years." "Californians Shun Vouchers," *NEA Today,* December 1993, p. 3.

[2] Deborah Edginton, manager of CTA's Instruction and Professional Development Department, *CTA Action* 30, no. 4 (December 1991).

5. It hurts minority students.
6. It violates the separation of church and state.
7. It will destroy the government schools.
8. It will destroy the independent schools.
9. It will lead to educational and cultural balkanization.

Not one of these charges is valid, but they resurface in almost every campaign for school choice. This chapter responds to each. Opponents of choice will use the same arguments in any state where a choice plan is proposed in the legislature or on the ballot.

Regulation of School Quality

Opponents of Proposition 174, blithely ignoring its text, insisted that under the initiative any slick operator, no matter how unqualified, could open an unregulated independent school and start collecting state money. CTA president Del Weber charged that "storefront schools will be popping up anywhere and everywhere, teaching God knows what," including white supremacy.[3] CEAV spokesman Rick Manter claimed that "a science course could be teaching kids how to make Molotov cocktails."[4] A barrage of negative advertising echoed these assertions. Three days before the election, the *Los Angeles Times* reported:

> With an unceasing flow of television and radio commercials, opponents of the school voucher initiative, Proposition 174 on Tuesday's state ballot, have conjured up images of "virtually anyone" opening tax-supported schools with "no real standards for teachers, no real course requirements."
>
> Polls show that the message has struck a chord with voters, who cite the lax regulation of private schools as one reason they are disinclined to support the measure.[5]

The rhetoric bore no resemblance to reality. Paragraphs (b)(1) and (b)(2) of the initiative prohibit any school that practices racial

[3]William Trombley, "Educators Group Calls School Voucher Ballot Proposal 'Evil,'" *Los Angeles Times*, 22 January 1992, p. A3.

[4]Philipp M. Gollner, "On the California Ballot: Should the State Help Pay for Private-School Pupils?" *New York Times*, August 4, 1993, p. B9. California Penal Code, section 11460, prohibits teaching the assembly of or demonstrating the use of any explosive or destructive device while knowing or intending that it be used to cause civil disorder.

[5]Jean Merl, "Keeping Standards," *Los Angeles Times*, October 30, 1993, p. A38 (Orange County edition).

discrimination or that advocates unlawful behavior from redeeming scholarships. Paragraph (b) incorporates existing state law governing independent schools, covering such matters as health and safety, personnel, curriculum, and graduation requirements. Paragraphs (a)(6), (b)(1), (b)(2), (b)(3), and (b)(5) authorize or impose additional standards. The media diligently reported the rhetoric; unfortunately, they rarely performed even a perfunctory reality check on it.

Dr. John Dean, superintendent of schools for Orange County, feared that the prospect of profit would attract unsavory entrepreneurs:

> I suppose since the initiative provides that anybody with 25 or more students can open a private school, and there are very few regulations on it, I think we're going to see them sprouting up all over the place, as entrepreneurs think this is a good way to make a few dollars. At $2,500 a year, with a classroom of 25 students, you're looking at $62,500 for nine months' work! That doesn't look too bad.[6]

Dr. Dean makes five mistakes. First, his estimate is low. The minimum initial scholarship value would have been $2,621, so a class of 25 students would generate revenue of $65,525. Of *course* that gets the attention of entrepreneurs, who must wonder why it takes twice that much—$131,050—for the government school system to educate the very same class. If the tuition voucher seems like a lot of money, it is only because government education is profoundly inefficient.

Second, Dr. Dean has apparently not attempted to open an independent school lately. It's not as easy as he thinks. In a *Los Angeles Times* interview, the Rev. Charles Rowins, president of the California Association of Private School Organizations,

> added that the notion of new schools—especially fly-by-night institutions—springing up to meet the demands of parents newly equipped with tuition vouchers is unfounded. Starting a new school—finding a site and complying with zoning, building, health and safety regulations, raising money and hiring a staff—is "very serious and difficult," he said.[7]

[6]"Parents, It's Your Choice," interview hosted by Bob and Geri Boyd, of Costa Mesa, California, on their syndicated radio show "Issues in Education," April 25, 1992.

[7]Merl, p. A41.

Third, how many fraudulent schools would it take to siphon $4 million in state money? That's the amount embezzled by Stephen Wagner, the top finance officer of the Newport-Mesa Unified School District. Wagner's was "the largest embezzlement of school funds in state history," according to the *Times*—the largest, but not the only. Surely Dr. Dean is aware of the case; Wagner's district falls under Dr. Dean's jurisdiction, and Wagner was convicted only a year before the school choice vote. Talk about fast operators. Apparently some of them work in government.[8]

Fourth, the initiative requires the state to prohibit the redemption of scholarships by any school that provides false or misleading information about itself. It also authorizes civil and criminal penalties for fraud in the solicitation of students or the redemption of scholarships.[9] There are easier ways for con artists—and entrepreneurs, for that matter—to make money than by founding a scholarship-redeeming school.

Fifth, Dr. Dean blithely assumes that anyone can get 25 students into a start-up school. Underlying that assumption is bureaucratic paternalism: if we let parents choose schools, they won't choose good ones. On the contrary, parents motivated enough to leave the government school system in search of a better education for their children are highly unlikely prey for new operators with no track record. Former secretary of education Bill Bennett writes:

> The education Establishment is still powerful, but it is intellectually bankrupt. It offers no serious ideas on how to reform and improve American education. None. And now it has become a merchant of fear. In the increasingly shrill world of the NEA [National Education Association] and the CTA, allowing parents to pick the schools their children will attend raises the specter of "David Koresh High School," science courses in which students learn how to make Molotov cocktails, witches' covens, etc.
>
> There are, of course, existing provisions to prevent these things from happening. More revealing is the mindset it exposes: Parents, left to themselves, would allow awful

[8]Lily Dizon, "Scandal Brought Big Changes to Newport-Mesa," *Los Angeles Times*, October 25, 1993, p. B1 (Orange County edition).

[9]As a young attorney, my first pro bono cases involved monolingual Hispanic immigrants who had been bilked by useless trade-tech schools. The initiative is designed to deter such fraud.

things to be done to their children. The unions' patronizing attitude toward parents is: We know better. The record clearly shows otherwise.[10]

The education establishment complained that the initiative did not require teachers in independent schools to be credentialed. In the words of Dr. John Dean, "There are no regulations for credentialing at all. I mean, the person who does this doesn't even have to be a college graduate."[11]

John Taylor Gatto explains the miracle of credentialing in his book *Dumbing Us Down*. Early in Gatto's career as a substitute teacher, he was sent to an eighth-grade typing class of 75 students. He was given no lesson plan, just one command: "Under no circumstances are you to allow them to type. You lack the proper license. Is that understood?"[12] The strict credentialing requirements followed by that school required the students to sit for an hour in a room with 75 typewriters but forbade them from typing. Certification is merely a clumsy regulatory means to a desired end, that of ensuring qualified teachers. A better means to the end is empowering parents to determine for themselves whether or not the teachers are doing their jobs.

The requirement of teacher credentialing is just as absent from California's new charter schools bill as from Proposition 174, but the education establishment never made an issue of that. Many people from nonacademic professions have training or experience that equips them to be superb teachers. In California, for example, highly qualified aerospace engineers are unemployed because of defense industry layoffs. Many would make good math and science teachers, which the state desperately needs. It makes no sense to bar them from the classroom simply because they lack a state credential.

Certification and regulation are not the answer. If standards and regulations demanding quality actually produced it, our government school system would have quality to burn. Go to any large law library, and you can find several feet of shelf space devoted to a set of rules called the California Education Code. The administrative

[10]William J. Bennett, "Prop. 174 Puts the Students First," *Los Angeles Times*, October 19, 1993, p. B11 (Orange County edition).

[11]"Parents, It's Your Choice."

[12]John Taylor Gatto, *Dumbing Us Down* (Philadelphia: New Society Publishers, 1992), p. 45.

rules and county and local policies promulgated under its authority take up several more feet of shelf space. Is more of the same going to guarantee quality? Not likely.

The best guarantor of quality is a parent with the power to take his or her child out of a school that isn't working. Parents don't need degrees in educational administration to know whether their children are being challenged academically. Parental empowerment is a far more effective motivator than regulation. Thus, even if the charge that independent schools are unregulated were true, it would not be decisive. The charge, however, is false.

Aid to the Rich

Opponents charge that school choice is simply a scheme to subsidize the tuition bills of the wealthy whose children are already in independent schools. They balk at spending $2,600 of public funds to send a rich kid to an independent school. Why, then, do they not balk at spending twice that amount to send the same student to a government school? They criticize the Parental Choice in Education Initiative for not means-testing scholarship recipients. Why, then, do they not criticize the absence of means testing from the government school system?

Over 20 years ago, in *Serrano* v. *Priest*,[13] the California Supreme Court held that the state constitution required equalizing funding among rich and poor school districts. In *Butt* v. *State*,[14] the court reaffirmed *Serrano* and went further, indicating that the constitution requires equality of educational opportunity as well as of funding. The Parental Choice in Education Initiative is the only proposal that fulfills that mandate. Far from favoring rich parents and rich schools, school choice takes opportunities presently enjoyed primarily by the rich and extends them to low- and middle-income families.

School choice is profoundly egalitarian. Its fundamental premise is that all children, just by virtue of being human, deserve the opportunity for a good education. If you're a school-age child, you qualify for the scholarship, period. There are no means tests, no academic qualifications, no other devices to divide, classify, and sort. Under the present system, the quality of education available to a school-age child depends largely on where he or she resides, which in

[13]*Serrano* v. *Priest*, 5 Cal.3d 584 (1971).
[14]*Butt* v. *State*, 93 Daily Journal D.A.R. 152 (1992).

turn depends in considerable part on income and race. Under the initiative, every child can claim a scholarship of equal value; every child has an equal right, once district enrollment assignments are complete, to enter any government school. The initiative offers the opportunity to choose among schools to high-, middle-, and low-income families alike.

Low-Income Students

Scholarship Amount vs. Independent School Costs

Fresno County superintendent of schools Pete Mehas, a sincere and likable representative of the education establishment, phrases his objection this way:

> Do I believe that the schools are failing many of our children? Absolutely I do. Does [the] system need radical reform? It does. Do I believe in parental choice? Absolutely. The more we empower parents, the greater the results would be. . . . But if you give somebody $2,600 and you have a private school with an average cost of $6,600, where is the poor person going to get that difference in tuition?[15]

I would share Pete's concern if his numbers were right. Although often cited, the $6,600 figure is inaccurate. As Chapter 5 explains, the U.S. Department of Education calculates the average cost of all independent schools nationwide at $2,000 per year. Even in high-cost California, the average independent school tuition appears to be less than the $2,600 scholarship amount. Thus the scholarship is more than sufficient to enable a student to pay for a good independent school.

Uninformed Parents

Opponents argue that some parents will make unwise choices, or no choice at all. Of course those who voice this concern are never speaking of themselves; it's always someone else who won't choose wisely. Michael Williams, formerly of the U.S. Department of Education, rejects the argument. He tells of growing up with a mother who worked as a maid and a father who drove trucks and did manual labor. Neither of his parents went beyond the sixth grade, but they wanted their son to go to college. From Midland, Texas,

[15]"Vouchers: Empowering or Crippling?" *Fresno Bee*, March 1, 1992, p. B5.

they sent him far away to El Paso so that he could attend a good school, which happened to be Catholic. "Even parents who have nothing," he says, "want their children to do better. They will do *anything* to get their children into a good school."[16] He suggests that the "some parents aren't smart enough to choose well" argument is condescending and paternalistic, if not racist.

Fortunately, it is also contrary to the evidence from existing school choice programs, where poor parents have grasped their newfound choice enthusiastically and exercised it intelligently. Choice engages parents in the educational process before classes even start: they learn about alternative schools, select one, and enroll their child there. At enrollment, the school can require them to help with homework, commit to a monthly conference, limit television on weekdays, or do any number of things to become involved with the work of the school and the education of the student. The East Harlem experience described in Chapter 10 is especially instructive. Parents there were as apathetic and uninvolved as could be; but once they were given signficant authority and responsibility, they began to exercise them.

Still, some children have apathetic or irresponsible parents. Obviously if the Parental Choice in Education Initiative could guarantee every child two responsible parents in a loving home, it would work wonders far beyond the classroom. But it can't do that. It can't outlaw apathy and ignorance. The initiative does not purport to cure all the ills of society. It simply offers options to people willing to exercise them.

Even so, children of uncaring parents are likely to be better off under the initiative. If other parents are exercising their choice to take their children out of poor schools, fewer children are left. Perhaps with a class of 25 instead of 35, the teacher can give more one-on-one attention. Further, a school that begins losing students to competitors will be motivated to improve. Relatively few well-informed parents who move their children can cause improvements that will benefit children of less involved parents as well.

Limited Enrollment Capacity

Michael Kilbourn of the Orange County Office of Education argued in a radio interview that independent schools have very

[16]Speech at black empowerment conference, Compton, Calif., January 30, 1992.

limited capacity. Low-income parents who want to transfer their children into independent schools will find that there is simply no room, he said. Later in the same interview, however, responding to a different question, Mr. Kilbourn argued that the initiative would destroy the government schools by causing a mass exodus of their best students. If there is no room for them in the independent schools, where are they going?

Kilbourn's superior, Dr. Dean, provided the answer: new independent schools will be "sprouting up all over the place." Independent school capacity is not static; it is already increasing to meet increasing demand. If tuition vouchers unleash pent-up demand for independent school space, they will also help provide the wherewithal to finance expansion.

The real capacity crunch is coming in the government school system, where California voters can't pass multibillion-dollar bond issues fast enough to accommodate the 40 percent enrollment growth—nearly two million additional students—anticipated from 1991 to 2000 under the state's own projections. Does it not make sense to allow the private sector to shoulder some of that burden? Glenn Noreen, business manager of the Fairmont private schools in Orange County, contrasts government and independent school construction costs. His local government school district claims that new school construction will cost $20,000 per unit of student capacity. Fairmont, which has four campuses, is constructing a fifth school at a per-student cost *80 percent lower:* $4,000 per unit of student capacity.[17]

Many fine parochial schools in the inner cities are in danger of closing their doors for financial reasons, even as nearby government schools suffer overcrowding. Joe McElligott, director of education for the California Catholic Conference, estimates that parochial schools statewide could absorb a 20 percent increase in enrollment without new construction. Leaders of other independent school associations give similar estimates. That means that existing independent school facilities could accommodate another 100,000 students.

True, with tuition vouchers, demand would far outrun that initial supply. But that only shows that capacity constraints affect the independent schools as well as the goverment schools. The real issue is which system can add capacity most efficiently.

[17]Telephone interview of Glenn Noreen, August 5, 1993.

Special Education Students

Opponents charge that the initiative is elitist because it permits independent schools to reject "undesirable" students. Exclusive independent schools, they allege, will take the cream of the crop, leaving the less fortunate students to fend for themselves. A typical example of this argument comes from Dr. John Dean, superintendent of public schools for Orange County, in an interview with Bob Boyd.

> Dean: The thing that concerns me as much as the money is, it's a discrimination issue. These choice schools can eliminate special ed kids, those who are not making appropriate progress. . . .
> Boyd: Like special students, maybe, with learning disabilities?
> Dean: That's right, they would all be rejected by the private schools.[18]

Dr. Dean's prophecy would come as a great surprise to the large membership of CAPSES, the California Association of Private Special Education Schools; to my friend Batia Nadler, whose independent Shachar Academy accepts only students with learning disabilities; to Matt Harris, whose Project Impact accepts only troubled kids; and to a host of independent school operators around the state who take pride in serving the students who most need help.

Del Weber, president of the CTA, complains that the initiative does not force independent schools to accept low-income students or those with disabilities. "The net result [will be] a large number of youngsters—perhaps 25% to 40%—for whom no school will be left, who will be 'throwaway kids,'" Weber predicts. "We call that evil."[19] Talk about throwaway kids: under the status quo that Weber defends, one out of five students drops out of school altogether, and two out of five graduate with the equivalent of a seventh-grade education. It would be hard for things to get worse.

Aside from that, though, Weber is simply wrong. Students with disabilities already *have* the equivalent of a voucher system. They have the right, under state law, to receive an adequate education regardless of the nature of their disabilities. Not all government schools are equipped to provide such an education, so what do they

[18]"Parents, It's Your Choice."
[19]Trombley, p. A3.

do about it? They contract with private providers![20] The initiative does nothing to limit that practice; in fact, it affirms the practice and extends its availability to all children. The initiative does nothing to limit the rights of low-income students or those with disabilities; rather, it expands their options and opportunities.

Minority Students

Representatives of the California Teachers Association, the California School Boards Association, the Association of California School Administrators, the California Federation of Teachers (AFL-CIO), the California School Employees Association, and various other education establishment and government employee groups charge that the initiative will fund white supremacy schools, that it will further white flight, and that it will lead to increased segregation.[21] Each allegation is false.

Paragraphs (b)(1) and (b)(2) of the initiative flatly prohibit the redemption of scholarships by any school that discriminates on the basis of race, that teaches hatred of any race, or that advocates unlawful behavior, including behavior based on prohibited racial discrimination.

As for white flight, the argument is a few decades too late. Where will the whites flee from? In the big urban school districts, most of them are already gone. As for those remaining, where will they flee to? The Catholic schools, where so-called minorities are a majority? Former secretary of education Bill Bennett states:

> I predict that any state that adopts choice will show a net *increase* in integration. Nationally, Catholic schools, which are private and parochial, are more integrated than public schools because residential living patterns result in *de facto* segregation. In all the choice programs we've seen around the country . . . we have seen a net increase in integration. That's because if you make the academic offerings attractive, almost everyone is going to want them regardless of race.[22]

[20]"Other public districts pay private schools to educate children who are disabled or have other special needs." Elizabeth Shogren, "A Chance to See Choice at Work," *Los Angeles Times*, October 22, 1993, pp. A1, A16 (Orange County edition).

[21]Trombley, p. A3; and Diana Walsh, "Push for School Vouchers," *San Francisco Examiner*, January 21, 1992, p. A-1.

[22]William J. Bennett, "An Obligation to Educate," *California Political Review*, Summer 1992, p. 35; emphasis in original.

In my travels as president of the Excellence through Choice in Education League (ExCEL), I rarely met rich white suburban Republicans who were desperate for alternative schools. It was always the inner-city pastors and parents who were most fervent in their support. They saw choice as their only educational hope. The *Los Angeles Times* tells of one such parent, Marvin Jackson, a father of five in south central Los Angeles. He supported Proposition 174,

> which he believes would grant him more control over the education of his children and the way the state spends his tax money.
>
> "I worked the 40-hour week; I paid the taxes. There should be some responsibility to listen to what I say," Jackson said. "This [initiative] is the first necessary step to bring about a much-needed change in public education in California. . . ."
>
> Many inner-city residents, usually staunch supporters of government institutions, believe the initiative would provide the shock the system needs to reform, forcing flagging campuses to improve through free-market competition with private and parochial schools. . . .
>
> Jackson, a 40-year-old father of five school-age youngsters from first grade to high school junior, does not envision immediately pulling his children out of the Los Angeles Unified School District and enrolling them in private institutions.
>
> But he does see himself, voucher in hand, marching into the school principal's office with a list of grievances to be addressed lest he take his business elsewhere.
>
> "The thing about the voucher is it could be used to get local control of our community schools," said Jackson, an electrical mechanic. "You take that voucher and you talk to the principal and you say, 'Let's get some real education going here. Let's get back to some reading, writing, and 'rithmetic. Let's get rid of condom distribution. If you want to experiment, get yourself some volunteers. Don't use my children.'"[23]

Marvin Jackson is precisely the sort of parent the drafters of the initiative intended to help. School choice will work best where the need for it is worst. As Adela de la Torre writes:

[23]Henry Chu, "Trading Places," *Los Angeles Times*, October 7, 1993, pp. A3, A32 (Valley edition).

114

For many Mexican-Americans and African-Americans, the issue of quality has forced re-evaluation of their commitment to public education. In the heart of Los Angeles or New York, the local parochial schools are filled with black and brown faces. That many parents in the urban core opt out of public education is not surprising, given the real fears that their children will not learn in an environment plagued with violence and with peer groups that negate the family values that they struggle to infuse in their children. Many working parents merely want their children to have a sanctuary for learning where common codes of behavior are assumed and teachers are not distracted from teaching. This is why, despite the economic hardship, many of these parents choose parochial schools—not because they do not believe in public education, but because they are not willing to gamble their children's future to prove that the system works. . . . Parents who care about their children and education are worth listening to, even if their voices do not echo those of the established power brokers.[24]

Separation of Church and State

Opponents of choice claim that the redemption of tax-funded tuition vouchers by church-sponsored schools would constitute state support of religion and thus would violate the federal Constitution. This is a serious concern, but not a valid one. The First Amendment simply states that "Congress shall make no law respecting an establishment of religion, or prohibiting the free exercise thereof. . . ." College students use government grants and loans to attend the schools of their choice, even if they are church sponsored, and no one raises constitutional objections. School choice simply lets parents of younger students do the same thing.

Those who attend college on the GI bill are welcome to choose church-affiliated or church-sponsored universities like Notre Dame, Yeshiva, Southern Methodist, Pacific Lutheran, Texas Christian, or Brigham Young. They can even study for the ministry if they want. The same is true of students using Pell grants, guaranteed student loans, and other state and federal aid. In so doing, they do not violate the Constitution any more than does a retiree whose dollar in the collection plate at church came from a Social Security check.

[24]Adela de la Torre, "Voucher Opponents Miss the Point," *Los Angeles Times*, October 20, 1993, p. B9 (Orange County edition).

In *Lemon* v. *Kurtzman*, the Supreme Court gave a three-part test for establishment-clause cases. To pass constitutional muster, challenged legislation must satisfy each of the three parts:

1. It must serve a secular purpose;
2. Its "primary effect" cannot be to advance or inhibit religion; and
3. It must not foster an "excessive entanglement" between religion and government.[25]

School choice passes all three parts of the test. It serves the secular purposes of improving educational quality and making a variety of educational options available to those who might not otherwise be able to afford them. Its primary effect is not to advance or inhibit religion but to create a free market in education. And it does not foster excessive entanglement between church and state.

Understandably, the Supreme Court generally disapproves of direct state aid to church-sponsored schools. However, the Court has repeatedly upheld the validity of programs in which state aid reaches such schools only indirectly, through individual choices. For example, in *Mueller* v. *Allen*, a 1983 case, the Court upheld income-tax deductions for educational expenses, including tuition at church-sponsored schools. The Court considered it significant that "aid to parochial schools is available only as a result of decisions by individual parents."[26] The First Amendment's establishment clause, noted Justice Rehnquist's opinion, "simply [does] not encompass the sort of attenuated financial benefit, ultimately controlled by the private choices of individual parents, that eventually flows to parochial schools" under an impartial tax-deduction program.[27] The same reasoning would sustain the Parental Choice in Education Initiative, which allows scholarships to be redeemed at any school, religious or not, and which grants scholarships to individual children through their parents rather than grants direct aid to any school.

In *Witters* v. *Department of Services for the Blind*, a 1986 case, the Court upheld the use of tax dollars at a Bible college. The challenged program allowed blind students to use vocational training funds to attend the vocational school of their choice, government or independent. One blind student wished to study for the ministry. The Court

[25]*Lemon* v. *Kurtzman*, 403 U.S. 602, 612–613 (1971).

[26]*Mueller* v. *Allen*, 463 U.S. 388, 399 (1983).

[27]*Mueller* v. *Allen*, 77 L.Ed.2d 721, 731 (1983).

held, unanimously, that he could do so.[28] Recently the Court held that government funds could be used to pay an interpreter for a deaf student attending a Catholic school. The *Wall Street Journal* reported:

> In his opinion for the majority, Chief Justice William Rehnquist asserted that the interpreter would be part of a program "that distributes benefits neutrally to any child qualifying as 'handicapped,'" without regard to the type of school involved.
>
> The chief justice reasoned that such aid wouldn't amount to a "direct subsidy" to a religious school, which the high court previously has ruled impermissible. "Handicapped children, not sectarian schools, are the primary beneficiaries" of the subsidy, he added. Any financial advantage enjoyed by a religious school is the result of private choices by parents who send their child there, not of public policy, the chief justice wrote.[29]

The Parental Choice in Education Initiative carefully defines the scholarships it offers as grants-in-aid to the children through their parents, and not to the schools in which the children enroll. The initiative neither favors nor disfavors church-sponsored schools. The benefits it offers are distributed according to individual choices, without state direction. These factors should resolve any establishment-clause concerns. In fact, the initiative would be more likely to run afoul of the First Amendment if it *prohibited* church-sponsored schools from accepting scholarships. Such a prohibition would arguably violate the other religion clause of the First Amendment, the free-exercise clause.

Effect on Government Schools

Early in 1992, as ExCEL was circulating petitions to qualify the initiative for the ballot, teachers in at least five separate Southern California school districts stapled to homework and sent home with children a flier opposing our efforts. The flier bears a drawing of a schoolhouse with broken windows and missing bricks. Outside the school the American flag hangs upside down at half mast. "Please don't sign!" the flier exclaims. "It will destroy the public schools!"

[28]*Witters* v. *Department of Services for the Blind*, 474 U.S. 481 (1986).

[29]Paul Barrett, "Court's Ruling on Help for Deaf Student Cheers Backers of Parochial-School Aid," *Wall Street Journal*, June 21, 1993, p. A12.

That amusing piece of propaganda actually boosted signature gathering efforts. Parents were so upset at the use of their children as political pawns, and so perturbed at being taken for fools, that they called ExCEL's offices in record numbers requesting petitions, which we gladly sent.

Nevertheless, the charge persists. In fact, as the *Los Angeles Times* reports, it is the rallying cry of the education establishment: "A coalition of education organizations and state employee groups . . . attacked a school voucher initiative proposed for the November ballot as an 'evil' measure that would destroy the public schools."[30] When pressed for details, those making the charge usually invoked one of three perceived threats: the best students will leave the government schools; the government schools will not be competing on a level playing field; or the initiative will take money from the government schools.

The Exodus

Nowhere does the initiative compel or even urge parents to send their children to an independent school. In fact, it offers what ought to be a strong incentive to stay in a government school instead: government school students receive double the per capita funding. Notwithstanding that, the educrats predict a mass exodus of the best students, with government schools retaining only those who are tougher to educate.

If the best students can't wait to leave, what does that say about the quality of the schools? That is an argument *for* school choice, not against it. If the government schools are doing such a poor job of meeting the needs of the high achievers, then we ought to let them leave. Excellence in education can hardly come from suppressing the excellent students. The exodus argument sounds like the old East German regime talking about the Berlin Wall: if we take it down, everyone will leave. Exactly; that is precisely why it should come down.

School choice doesn't favor independent schools over government ones; it lets parents favor good schools over bad ones. A mass exodus will occur only if government school quality is significantly poorer than independent school quality. Are opponents admitting that that is the case? As education consultant and former teacher Martha

[30]Trombley, p. A3.

Brown says, "Since Day One of the choice movement we've heard laments that 'Choice will destroy public schools!' It sounds more convincing every year."[31] Parental choice cannot destroy the government school system; inferior quality can.

Fears of mass departures are probably overblown. Existing school choice programs, as the examples in Chapter 10 show, tend to serve not the best students but the most troubled. One who is doing well academically, athletically, or socially in the government schools has little incentive to leave. One who is having trouble is far more likely to benefit from an alternative. Moreover, as the examples in Chapter 5 show, the success of independent schools cannot be attributed to selective admissions. Many have low or no academic entrance requirements, and many proudly specialize in succeeding with troubled kids.

The Level Playing Field

Pete Mehas, superintendent of Fresno County schools, complains, "With this initiative, you are creating unfair competition. You're basically giving everyone $2,600 to go to the school of his or her choice, but public schools have to abide by all the state and federal regulations."[32] Harry Weinberg, superintendent of the San Diego County schools, demands a "level playing field"; he wants independent schools subjected to the same regulations that bind government schools.[33]

Let me get this straight: state regulation is so overwhelming that even with double the per-student funding, government schools are at a disadvantage—and Weinberg's solution is to create more regulation? The educators say their hands are tied by regulation. The initiative, through the charter school provision in subsection (c), offers a way for government schools to escape such regulation. The educrats reply that they would rather tie everyone else's hands than untie their own.

Competition is always unsettling to those who have been shielded from it. But there are good people in the government system, and we have confidence in their ability to compete. The initiative's goal

---

[31]Martha Brown, "School Choice Foes Defend the Indefensible," *Wall Street Journal,* June 25, 1992.

[32]"Vouchers: Empowering or Crippling?" p. B5.

[33]Quoted in Brown.

is to free all schools, government and independent, from regulations that get in their way. Government schools as well as independent ones will be enabled to compete more effectively.

A variation on the level playing field argument is the plea that we restrict choice to government schools only. Pete Mehas again: "Let's say we should have choice within the public school system. We're going to deregulate the schools, we're going to put dollars into the classroom where they belong instead of into district offices. Half the county offices that don't work for us should be eliminated even if it means my own county office. Let's put the dollar into the classroom. . . . If it doesn't work, I say amen."[34]

Those are good ideas—so good that one wonders why only the threat of the Parental Choice in Education Initiative prompted the education establishment to consider them. Why aren't those reforms happening now? Without the initiative, they might be discussed. Under the initiative, they will be implemented, and quickly. Parental choice will virtually force the government schools to adopt such reforms to become competitive.

Dr. Mehas is on a slippery slope. He admits that parents should have choice—as long as they choose his schools. He admits that deregulation is necessary—as long as the government school system keeps its monopoly on tax-funded education. He admits that dollars should go to the classroom instead of the bureaucracy—but opposes the initiative, the only plan that lets parents do an end run around the bureaucracy. Letting parents choose any school as long as it's a government school is like letting them eat at any restaurant as long as it's a McDonald's or buy any car as long as it's made by General Motors.

Fiscal Impact

Opponents claimed that the initiative would cost taxpayers billions of dollars and would take money away from the government schools. Bill Bennett responds to the first claim:

> School choice makes economic sense. Three Nobel laureates, more than 140 leading economists and every major anti-tax group in California have endorsed Proposition 174. Independent analyses conclude that the more people use vouchers, the more money the taxpayers will save. Increased

[34]"Vouchers: Empowering or Crippling?" p. B5.

120

private school enrollment will also reduce the need to build hundreds of new public schools to accommodate the 1.8 million new students who are expected to enter the system by the year 2000.[35]

The second claim (that the initiative would take money from the government schools) takes some explaining. On March 17, 1992, I traveled to Sacramento with a delegation from the organization Agudath Israel to meet, among others, state superintendent of public instruction Bill Honig. Knowing that Agudath Israel favored the Parental Choice in Education Initiative, Honig spent the meeting bashing it. His primary objection was that the initiative "takes $5,000 to $10,000 per kid from the public schools."[36] "Whoever drafted this initiative was either nasty, malicious, or incompetent," he said. "They didn't have the guts to say that somebody has to pay."

For a $2,600 scholarship to take $5,000 to $10,000 from the government schools is indeed an impressive feat of new math. How does it allegedly happen? Honig argues that paragraph (b)(8) of the initiative eviscerates Proposition 98's minimum school-funding guarantee by subtracting, for every independent school student, $2,600 for the scholarship, another $2,600 in savings, and $5,200 in ADA (average daily attendance) money. "All this," he scowled, "when we're already so starved for funds."

(Reader Advisory: Even lawyers and economists will find the remainder of this subsection dry. Unless you are keenly interested in California school finance law, skip to the next section.)

Honig's interpretation of the initiative is incorrect. His charge is inconsistent with both the intent and the language of the initiative, as well as the structure of Proposition 98. The Parental Choice in Education Initiative neither repeals nor significantly weakens Proposition 98; it merely modifies 98 to accommodate the parental choice program. As Chapter 6 explains, Proposition 98 sets forth multiple formulas for determining the minimum level of spending on the government school system, including the community colleges; the state is required to apply whichever formula generates the highest number. Generally the state must spend either

[35]Bennett, "Prop. 174 Puts the Students First," p. B11.

[36]At the time, Honig himself was taking money from the schools through a creative and illegal enterprise, for which he was later convicted and removed from office. The irony apparently escaped him.

- (Test 1) the amount that equals the percentage of the general fund spent on the government school system in 1986–87 (approximately 42 percent of the general fund) or
- (Tests 2 and 3) an amount matching or exceeding the prior year's spending, adjusted for enrollment growth and inflation.

The initiative's fiscal goal is to make the dollar follow the scholar. Current annual per capita spending on the government school system is $5,200. The initiative intends for a student who remains in the government school system to continue receiving $5,200 in funding. If the student leaves the government school system, the $5,200 should also leave. Of the $5,200 that leaves, $2,600 (or more, if the legislature so determines) goes to the scholarship. The remainder reverts to the state's general fund, where it is available for use as the legislature sees fit. That money could cover existing independent school students when they are phased in and could pay for the special education and transportation grants authorized in paragraph (a)(2) of the initiative. The program is intended to be self-funding, with no new cost to the taxpayer.

Now assume that the initiative made no changes to Proposition 98. A student who transferred from a government to an independent school would get a $2,600 scholarship. But Test 1 would force the state to keep spending on the government school system as though the student were still there! The taxpayers would have to pay twice for the student's education: once for an education he wasn't even getting in the government schools and again for the scholarship. No matter how many students left the government schools, Proposition 98 would require the state to keep funding the system as though they had all stayed.

Thus, the first sentence of paragraph (b)(8) of the initiative says, "Expenditures for scholarships issued under this Section and savings resulting from the implementation of this Section shall count toward the minimum funding requirements for education established by Sections 8 and 8.5 of Article XVI." Translated into English, that means that when the student leaves the government school system, so does $5,200. That $5,200 counts toward Proposition 98, and logically so: $2,600 or more goes toward the scholarship; the remainder, most likely, will fund scholarships for existing independent school students, special education students, and so on.

That takes care of Test 1. But remember that Proposition 98 requires the state to spend the *highest* amount generated by the alternative formulas. Tests 2 and 3 would still operate. If "enrollment growth" in Tests 2 and 3 were interpreted to include enrollment in independent as well as government schools, then again Proposition 98 would force the state to keep giving money to the government school system for students no longer in it. Thus, the second sentence of paragraph (b)(8) of the initiative says, "Students enrolled in scholarship-redeeming schools shall not be counted toward enrollment in public schools and community colleges for purposes of Sections 8 and 8.5 of Article XVI." In other words, Tests 2 and 3 cannot count independent school students toward the government school funding minimum.

Paragraph (b)(8) of the Parental Choice in Education Initiative simply says that government schools don't get money for students not attending them. This provision ensures that the educational dollar (1) follows the scholar and (2) counts toward Proposition 98's minimum funding requirement, whether it is spent in government or independent schools. Without this provision, Proposition 98 would require the state to pay the government schools to educate students who had already transferred to independent schools; the taxpayers would be double-billed. The initiative does not affect per-student spending in the government school system. The fiscal impact argument is a red herring.[37]

Effect on Independent Schools

Many independent school operators fear that if they accept state scholarships from their students, state regulation will inevitably follow. Dave Rolph, school superintendent for Calvary Chapel Costa Mesa, personally favored the initiative but had reservations. "The courts will decide that if anyone in your school receives this scholarship, then your school is under the control of the state government," he says. "It is so important for us to be independent. Unless there

---

[37]The initiative could repeal Proposition 98 altogether without affecting actual school appropriations. Proposition 98, passed by the barest of majorities in 1988, merely sets a minimum level of funding. The legislature provided ample funding to the schools long before Proposition 98 was enacted, and since then the legislature has provided funding in excess of the minimum. The initiative does not, and indeed cannot, "take money away from the public schools." Only the legislature appropriates tax dollars.

is a guarantee of no control, we can't accept the scholarships. I would hate to do that to our families. But what we teach is none of the state's business, and we want it to stay that way."[38]

Some independent school parents who would like to support vouchers hesitate when they hear charges that state aid will destroy the independence of independent schools. If the initiative allowed the state to regulate independent education into the same pit as government education, then it might do more harm than good. The drafters of the initiative were keenly aware of this concern. They consulted with attorneys for various home, religious, and other independent school associations throughout the drafting process. Not coincidentally, the initiative carefully protects independent schools—whether they choose to accept scholarships or not—from additional state and local regulation.

It does so through 10 key provisions. First, the initiative defines the scholarships as grants to the children through their parents, and not to the schools. The legal importance of this distinction is discussed earlier in this chapter, in the analysis of church-and-state issues, and also in Chapter 6, in the comment on paragraph (a)(4).

Second, the initiative becomes part of the California Constitution, the fundamental law of the state; and it overrides any contrary constitutional provision or interpretation. Some independent school operators fear a repeat of the *Grove City* case, which held that colleges who admitted students accepting federal financial aid thereby became subject to federal regulation. But there is an important difference: in that dispute, no federal constitutional provision explicitly protected independent school independence. Under the initiative, the California Constitution will.

Third, the initiative reserves the individual schools' right to choose which tests they will administer. The state is not authorized to impose any particular tests, standards, or outcome requirements on the schools.

Fourth, the state education bureaucracy has no authority to deny scholarship-redeeming status to any independent school, as long as that school is in compliance with legal requirements existing as of October 1, 1991, and with the requirements of the initiative. Independent schools do not need state permission to redeem scholarships;

[38]"Parents, It's Your Choice."

they become scholarship-redeeming schools simply by filing a statement indicating that they comply with the requirements above.

Fifth, new regulation at the state level requires a three-fourths vote of the state legislature—a very high hurdle. Independent schools lack such protection. Today at both the state and local level, a mere majority can impose new regulation.

Sixth, new regulation at the local level requires a two-thirds vote of the governing body, plus a majority vote of the people—again, a uniquely high hurdle.

Seventh, in any legal proceeding arising out of these provisions, the *government* bears the burden of establishing that the regulation is *essential*—essential to the health, safety, or education of students, not merely essential to the government—and does not burden independent schools unduly. Taken together, these provisions mean that new regulation can occur only when there is virtually universal societal consensus. That is far greater protection than independent schools enjoy today *without* the parental choice scholarships.

Eighth, the initiative reaffirms the right of any school to impose a code of conduct and discipline and enforce it with sanctions, including dismissal.

Ninth, the initiative requires the state to disburse scholarship funds in equal amounts monthly; independent schools won't be left hanging.

Tenth, the initiative includes carefully drafted provisions that minimize the risk of legal challenges' delaying the program and that make these provisions severable in the unlikely event that any such challenge is successful.

In summary, rather than threaten the independence of independent schools, the initiative carefully and thoroughly protects them.

The Common Culture

Opponents charge that under school choice independent schools, particularly religious ones, will promote their own agendas and viewpoints rather than strengthen our common American culture and values. Morton Kondracke writes:

> Sometimes in an effort to teach tolerance, educators end up promoting separatism. But the same result can flow from the conservative "choice" agenda if Jewish parents use public funds to send their kids to Orthodox schools, Protestant

> fundamentalists to Christian schools, African-Americans to
> Afrocentric schools, Latinos to Spanish-language schools,
> and Catholics to Catholic schools. . . . Balkanization of Ameri-
> can society is a real danger.[39]

Kondracke expresses a legitimate and serious concern. However,
it is precisely the failure of the government schools to transmit our
common American culture and values that deeply concerns many
parents. Is Kondracke suggesting that students currently attending
Orthodox, Catholic, and other independent schools are less versed
in the common culture or less tolerant than their government school
peers? Such a position is untenable. Besides, "freedom to choose
one's own agenda" is "at the core" of the American democratic
tradition, writes education consultant and former teacher Martha
Brown, and parental choice

> allows parents who wish to do so to reject the public school
> agenda, which—at taxpayer expense—often substitutes
> counseling for education and teaches values many believe
> to be in conflict with the family, morality, and free en-
> terprise. . . . We all lose when everyone is forced to accept
> government decisions for fear of "inequalities" if people
> make their own.[40]

I once heard California superintendent of public instruction Bill
Honig admit, in a private meeting, that the government schools
were utterly failing to foster character development and provide
moral education. He admitted that 90 percent of Californians agreed
that schools needed to teach moral values and that the government
schools were not doing so. His proposed solution: spend more
money on teacher training![41] Batia Nadler said to him, "But in the
public schools, I can't even mention the *reason* to be ethical: God.
In my school, I teach my children that I am a reflection of my creator."
"We don't have that luxury in the public schools," Honig replied.
"Exactly!" said Batia. "That's the problem!"
Can independent schools promote their own religious viewpoints,
their own philosophies? Of course, and that is a healthy thing. We

[39]Morton M. Kondracke, "Pennsylvania Avenue," *Roll Call*, July 5, 1993, pp. 7, 11.
[40]Brown.

[41]Honig made these remarks in a colloquy with Batia Nadler in the California state
senate chamber while meeting with a delegation from Agudath Israel on March 17,
1992. I have detailed notes of their exchange.

Americans pay a great deal of lip service to "diversity," although we usually mean only diversity of race or color. Diversity of thought is healthy too. We have nothing to fear from a free market of ideas, where participants have to rely on persuasion rather than compulsion. That is one of the most fundamental American values of all.

8. "Fight It Fang and Claw": The Attack on Proposition 174

California's First "Anti-Signature" Campaign

To place a constitutional initiative on California's statewide ballot requires the signatures of over 615,000 registered voters. The Excellence through Choice in Education League (ExCEL) began circulating signature petitions late in December of 1991. In January of 1992 ExCEL began receiving reports of incidents in which individuals identifying themselves as California Teachers Association (CTA) members threatened signature gatherers and harassed voters attempting to sign the petitions. CTA members were not merely exercising their freedom of speech; they were forcing themselves between signers and petition circulators, picking arguments with people who had already signed the petitions, and even forming human chains to prevent people from signing. At one San Diego location, 12 CTA members surrounded a solitary petitioner. In San Francisco, two CTA members demanded that a petitioner hand over his school choice signatures to them. Within days, similar incidents were reported in San Marcos, Fullerton, Westminster, Thousand Oaks, Huntington Beach, and Sacramento.

Questioned by reporters, a CTA official admitted hiring Kimball Petition Management, Inc., to report the location of ExCEL's signature gatherers and to advise the CTA on how to impede their work. Never before had opponents of an initiative attempted to prevent voters from even placing it on the ballot. In February, the *Los Angeles Times* reported:

> CTA officials acknowledged that volunteers are confronting prospective petition signers, urging them not to sign, but said their methods are "educational, not physical." ... Ned Hopkins, CTA assistant executive director, said his organization and other education groups opposed to the Parental

Choice Initiative have dispatched groups of "leafleteers" to try to persuade people not to sign the petitions.

"Are we trying to interfere with their ability to get enough signatures to qualify?" he asked. "Yes, that's our intention, there's no doubt about that." . . . He said the leaflet distributors have been trained to follow 15 rules, including "Do not threaten the petition pusher" and "Do not use a handle or stick on the poster or raise it above your shoulders."

"But that some individuals might get overzealous is not a surprise," Hopkins said. "That happens in every campaign."

He said the anti-voucher coalition has hired a signature-gathering company, Kimball Associates Petition Management of Tarzana, "to advise us." He said the firm has been hired specifically to keep the voucher initiative off the ballot, not for the usual reason of helping to qualify a measure.

"It's been very useful to us in knowing how to discourage potential signers," Hopkins said. "We go to places where they [Kimball's company] have indicated signature gatherers are likely to be."[1]

The CTA urged anyone who saw signatures being gathered to call a hotline so that the union could dispatch people to interfere.[2]

In its next newsletter the CTA boasted of its anti-signature campaign, and in April the *Times* reported:

the state's first "anti-signature" campaign is in full swing. . . . Leaflet-laden California Teachers Assn. members. . .have taken to the shopping centers, shadowing petition gatherers and attempting to persuade voters to withhold support. . . . Consequently, ExCEL has been forced to supplement its paid petitioning program by gathering signatures the old-fashioned way: volunteers. . . .

"The [public school teachers] can't get at the volunteers because they go door to door or talk to friends or whatever," said ExCEL President David J. Harmer. "That effort is picking up steam really nicely."[3]

Although ExCEL's volunteers did heroic work, collecting signatures door to door is not very efficient; we still needed to rely on

[1]William Trombley, "Effort to Sabotage School Voucher Petitions Alleged," *Los Angeles Times*, February 21, 1992, p. A3.

[2]Thomas Sowell, "Against Choice, the Empire Strikes Back," *Orange County Register*, April 22, 1992, p. B9.

[3]Paul Feldman, "No Lack of Initiative," *Los Angeles Times*, April 13, 1992, p. A3.

signature gatherers stationed in public places. But the CTA kept interfering with their work. "The justification offered at the 1992 NEA [National Education Association] convention by CTA President Del Weber," reports *Forbes*, was "frankly totalitarian: 'There are some proposals that are so evil that they should never even be presented to the voters.'"[4] Union to voters: Take a hike. We've already decided this issue for you.

Your Tax Dollars at Work

While the CTA was harassing signature gatherers, school boards began campaigning against the initiative. California law forbids spending public funds to support or oppose candidates or ballot measures,[5] but the California School Boards Association asked every school board in the state to publicly oppose the initiative.[6] Soon school boards were passing resolutions opposing the initiative and printing and distributing them at public expense. Most boards refused to allow representatives of ExCEL to speak. For that matter, some refused to allow *any* dissenter to speak. Columnist Harold Johnson of the *Orange County Register* wrote, "The First Amendment has been sent to the shredder by some school boards that have voted to oppose the initiative. I've heard from a couple of school trustees who've been told not to take issue publicly with the official position of their boards."[7]

The Los Angeles Unified School District (LAUSD) board, characteristically, was among the worst offenders. On March 2, 1992, the board devoted its meeting to campaigning against the initiative. All six board members present spoke against it, then passed a resolution opposing it. Mark Slavkin claimed that the initiative "is simply a subsidy to a few" and urged his fellow board members to go "on record and take a leadership role in communicating to see that this measure is defeated." Barbara Boudreaux said, "I would like to tell our viewing audience . . . please don't sign the initiative . . . oppose this destructive measure." Roberta Weintraub also urged viewers

---

[4]Peter Brimelow and Leslie Spencer, "The National Extortion Association?" *Forbes*, June 7, 1993, p. 79.

[5]*Stanson* v. *Mott*, 17 Cal.3d 206, 130 Cal. Rptr. 697 (1976).

[6]"Schoolyard Bullies," editorial, *Wall Street Journal*, March 18, 1992.

[7]Harold Johnson, "Schools Teach the ABCs of Machine Politics," *Orange County Register*, March 26, 1992, p. B13.

not to sign the initiative. Jeff Horton hoped "we can mount a strong enough campaign to keep it off the ballot and defeat it if it qualifies." Leticia Quezada called the initiative a "fraud" and a "lie," then restated her views in Spanish. Julie Korenstein predicted that the initiative would lead to "bigotry" and "a fascist type of society." She concluded, "I hope that everyone who is listening to Channel 58—and a lot of folks listen to our program—when a petitioner comes up to you, tell him you don't agree with that philosophy."[8]

Ladies and gentlemen, the prosecution rests: these buffoons have no business governing the education of anyone's children.

Not only did the LAUSD board utter the remarks above, it broadcast them in their entirety on at least two occasions—at public expense. Needless to say, ExCEL was not permitted to respond. ExCEL counsel Manny Klausner had to go to court to stop LAUSD from using Channel 58, its publicly funded and ostensibly educational cable television station, for political propaganda. Klausner also sued to stop similar abuses in several other districts, including Las Virgenes, Simi Valley, Saddleback Valley, and Alta Loma. In each of these cases, the courts issued injunctions forbidding further expenditures of public funds for impermissible campaigning.[9]

With the school boards neutralized, other organizations took up the fight, among them the California Parent-Teacher Association. State PTA vice president Grace Foster urged members to fight the initiative "fang and claw" and ordered them not to "give our enemy the platform" by allowing debates.[10] This was not mere rhetoric; the state PTA enforced Foster's order. The *Wall Street Journal* reported:

> A campaign of intimidation is also being waged to make people toe the public school party line. Kathy Moran, a PTA official in Villa Park, received a letter from the state organization demanding that PTA leaders "do everything possible" to block the gathering of signatures. When she tried to organize a debate on the merits of choice, she was told that PTA chapters must present only the anti-choice perspective.[11]

[8]Respondents' brief, *Choice in Education League* v. *Los Angeles Unified School District*, California Court of Appeal, 2nd Civ. No. B–067139, pp. 2–5.

[9]"The 'Evil' in California," editorial, *Wall Street Journal*, September 14, 1992, p. A12.

[10]Dan Froomkin, "Budget, Voucher Concerns Dominate PTA Opening Day," *Orange County Register*, May 16, 1992, pp. 1, 13.

[11]"Schoolyard Bullies."

Mrs. Moran held the debate anyway. Parents filled the school auditorium and listened intently. After the debate, in which I participated, many of them told me it was the first time they had been able to hear any arguments for the initiative.

Despite Klausner's legal victories against improper taxpayer-funded campaigning, schools and school employees continued opposing the initiative on school property, on school time, and at school expense. *Orange County Register* columnist Harold Johnson asked readers who had examples of campaigning by school employees to call him. "My phone's been ringing ever since," he reported. A few examples:

> A parent with kids at El Camino Real Elementary School in Irvine says they were given handouts in the form of oversized checks shouting that the choice plan is a "FRAUD." (As with many callers, this one requested I not name him, for fear of retaliation against his kids.)
>
> "Learn the facts—please don't sign," reads a mailer to parents at the George White Elementary School in Laguna Niguel. It includes 15 talking points that are "totally one-sided," a recipient groused to me.
>
> Robin Hyde of Yorba Linda, father of a student at Fullerton's Troy High School, complained about a [sic] anti-initiative article by the principal in the parent association's newsletter. "Total disinformation—not even close to balanced," said Hyde, whose wife happens to be a Placentia school district employee, and who added he hasn't made up his mind about the initiative. "I just don't think the schools have any business taking sides."
>
> A teacher in Norco reports "They're coming down big-time against the voucher" at his school, where brochures warning about "cult schools" can be found in the teachers' lounge.
>
> Principal Gary Ernst of Fountain Valley High School included a broadside against the initiative in his latest newsletter to parents.
>
> Georgia Albano of Upland opposes the choice initiative—but she's steamed that a PTA campaign sheet against it was handed out to her children at Valencia Elementary School.
>
> The PTA at Villa Park Elementary School is considering breaking ties with the statewide hierarchy, in part because they've been told they can't dissent from its opposition to the initiative. . . .

133

Diane Schwartz, a parent in Orange, asked the county Education Department to refer her to any codes that address political activity by school employees. She received a letter from department lawyer Ronald Wenkert, who said he couldn't divulge such information to "members of the general public." Attorney-client privilege, you know. Talk about arrogance: The agency's lawyers are saying they work for the schools establishment, not for Ms. Schwartz and the millions of other taxpayers who just happen to pay their salaries.[12]

Why the Public-Be-Damned Tactics?

Not content with harassing signature gatherers and using the schools as soapboxes, the education establishment offered Michael Arno, president of American Petition Consultants, a "retainer" of $400,000 if he agreed not to work for the initiative.[13] Some initiative opponents deliberately signed multiple petitions, distorting the signature count and invalidating the duplicate signatures. The *San Diego Union-Tribune* reported that many petition signers were

suspected of trying to scuttle the measure by deliberately signing the petitions more than once.

A full review of the duplicates conducted yesterday revealed that 32 people signed the petitions 10 or more times.

"We have many, many more than that who signed seven, eight or nine times," said Conny McCormack, registrar of voters for San Diego County. One person signed 23 times.

Altogether, McCormack said, of the 50,276 San Diego signatures disqualified in the final count completed Wednesday, 11,850 were scratched out because of duplications.

"That's a very high number of duplicates," the registrar said. "There is clearly more fraud here than we've ever seen before."[14]

Proponents intended to place the initiative on the November 1992 ballot. However, the high number of fraudulent signatures substantially delayed the verification process in several large counties. By the time the county registrars of voters finally certified that the

[12]Johnson, p. B13.

[13]"The 'Evil' in California," p. A12.

[14]Maura Reynolds, "School Voucher Initiative Qualifies for '94 Ballot," *San Diego Union-Tribune*, August 21, 1992, p. A3.

initiative had enough valid signatures to qualify, the deadline for the November 1992 ballot had passed. Voters would have to wait until the next statewide election.

CTA harassment of signature gatherers, school boards denouncing the initiative at public expense, school-based negative campaigning, the PTA's preventing proponents from speaking, the payoff offered to Arno, fraudulent signatures—this isn't the little red schoolhouse. Why these "public-be-damned tactics?" asks Thomas Sowell. Why was there "such an all-out effort to keep the school choice initiative off the ballot?" His answer:

> The educational establishment knows that any such re- forms have to be headed off at the pass, because once the public has a choice—and especially after it exercises that choice and sees the benefits to the children—there will be no stopping the demand for fundamental changes in the way our public schools function and malfunction. . . . Once people get a chance to see the difference with their own eyes, public schools are going to have to shape up or ship out. Some of the incompetent teachers and administrators currently enjoying iron-clad job protection and automatic raises are going to be in big trouble.
> Their own desperate efforts to keep the issue off the ballot in the first place betray their clear understanding that their hides are at stake because their schools cannot measure up to the competition.[15]

Employees of the government school system give all kinds of reasons why parents should not have choice, but the most fundamental is their fear that parents will choose independent schools. No bureaucracy surrenders money or power voluntarily. The education bureaucracy is no different. As John Chubb and Terry Moe explain, the most powerful political groups involved in education

> are those with vested interests in the current institutional system: teachers' unions and myriad associations of princi- pals, school boards, superintendents, administrators, and professionals—not to mention education schools, book pub- lishers, testing services, and many other beneficiaries of the institutional status quo.
> These groups are opposed to institutional change, or at least any such change that is truly fundamental. Current

[15]Sowell, p. B9.

arrangements put them in charge of the system, and their jobs, revenues, and economic security depend on keeping the basic governance structure pretty much as it is.[16]

Parental choice represents a life-or-death struggle to these groups, and they respond accordingly. In their campaign against Oregon's 1990 school choice initiative they ran television ads showing a classroom of children in Ku Klux Klan robes.[17] In California the educrats repeatedly linked the initiative to skinheads, white supremacist David Duke, and cult leader David Koresh.[18] Such desperate tactics, say Peter Brimelow and Leslie Spencer, reveal the education establishment's understanding that it cannot afford to lose—and its great fear that, in a civil campaign, it will lose.[19]

The November 1993 Campaign

Although excluded from the November 1992 ballot, the Parental Choice in Education Initiative went to a statewide vote a year later, in November of 1993. A month before the election the *Los Angeles Times* could still report a tight race: "A recent Times poll found voters closely divided on the issue, with 39% in favor and 45% opposed. Democrats were slightly more opposed than voters at large."[20] Proponents were within striking distance; clearly they could win.

Led by the CTA, the education establishment struck with a vengeance. The campaign to keep the initiative off the ballot was child's play compared to the campaign to defeat it once it was there. Fighting Proposition 174 were

[16]John E. Chubb and Terry M. Moe, *Politics, Markets and America's Schools* (Washington: Brookings Institution, 1990), pp. 11–12.

[17]David Boaz, "The Public School Monopoly: America's Berlin Wall," in *Liberating Schools: Education in the Inner City,* ed. David Boaz (Washington: Cato Institute, 1991), p. 47.

[18]See, for example, William Trombley, "Educators Group Calls School Voucher Ballot Proposal 'Evil,'" *Los Angeles Times,* January 22, 1992, p. A3; and Diana Walsh, "Push for School Vouchers," *San Francisco Examiner,* January 21, 1992, p. A-1. The first individual I heard raise the specter of Koresh—but not the last—was Michael Kilbourn of the Orange County Office of Education, in a radio debate taped on August 5, 1993.

[19]Brimelow and Spencer, p. 83.

[20]David Lauter, "Clinton Urges 'No' Vote on School Voucher Initiative," *Los Angeles Times,* October 5, 1993, p. A3 (Orange County edition).

seven unions and associations that comprise the public education establishment, according to the state [campaign spending] report released Tuesday [October 12].

The political arm of the California Teachers Assn. has given $8,489,128, while the California School Employees Assn. has given $1,010,375, the California Federation of Teachers $355,886 and the Assn. of California School Administrators $317,518.

Since August, voucher opponents have spent this money on radio and television ads attacking Proposition 174 as too risky and costly, and raising the possibility that tax money would be given to private schools that could discriminate against children.[21]

Proponents could not even remotely approach such institutional support and funding. "Statewide, voucher foes are outspending those backing the initiative at least 10 to 1," reported the *Times*.[22] The first (and only) pro-174 television commercial did not appear until three weeks before the election. At the press briefing introducing the commercial, campaign strategist Ken Khachigian had to admit that the campaign lacked the money to air more commercials. It is "a major, major disappointment that the business community has taken a walk on this campaign," he said.[23]

School Campaigning

Beyond the expenditures reported by the anti-174 campaign, government school officials continued lobbying the voters with their own tax dollars. California attorney general Dan Lungren had to warn the schools to quit using tax funds for their negative campaign:

Lungren cited questionable activities by some school officials, including a school superintendent in San Jose who wrote an anti-Proposition 174 message in a publicly funded newsletter. . . .

The attorney general sent general warning letters to all county school superintendents, cautioning them against violating election code provisions prohibiting the use of public funds or equipment for political causes.

[21]Jodi Wilgoren and Dan Morain, "O.C. Cash Helps Voucher Allies Air First TV Ad," *Los Angeles Times*, October 13, 1993, p. A1 (Orange County edition).

[22]Jodi Wilgoren, "Voucher Vitriol," *Los Angeles Times*, October 25, 1993, p. B1 (Orange County edition).

[23]Wilgoren and Morain, p. A1.

> He also sent copies of anti–Proposition 174 flyers distrib-
> uted by some schools to seven district attorneys.[24]

In response to Lungren's warning, government school districts changed the form of their campaigning, but not its substance. Rather than explicitly instructing voters to oppose the initiative, many school districts began giving them purportedly impartial analyses of its effects. Some districts announced draconian post-174 budgets and mailed them out at taxpayer expense. These budgets were abso-lute fantasies, but the media reported them with the faith of a child. Consider this typical news item:

> The Brea-Olinda Unified School District has unveiled plans to lay off teachers, librarians, high school counselors and other staff members and to eliminate programs if Proposition 174, the school voucher initiative, passes on the Nov. 2 ballot.
> District officials said Brea-Olinda will lose 10%, or $2 mil-lion, in funds if voters approve the measure.
> Cuts would include 10 teachers, eight clerks, two custodi-ans, the junior high guidance specialist, all four high school counselors, a district office staffer, about 10 bus drivers and all eight librarians.
> The elimination of librarian jobs—one at each of the dis-trict's eight libraries—would mean that no one could check out books because the libraries would be closed. . . .
> District officials mailed out a newsletter outlining the potential cuts to show parents how the initiative would affect their children's schooling.[25]

Vote for 174 and we'll have to fire the bus drivers and close the libraries! Throughout the state claims like these were published and distributed at taxpayer expense. The charges are asinine. The initiative doesn't even purport to set public school funding levels. Under the initiative, as before, the state legislature and local school boards would determine school funding in their annual budgets.

---

[24]Among the offending districts were Tustin Unified School District in Orange County and several others in Los Angeles and San Diego counties. Dan Morain, "Voucher Foes Cleared of Misusing Public Funds," *Los Angeles Times*, October 5, 1993, p. A27 (Orange County edition).

[25]"Schools Plan Layoffs If Prop. 174 Passes," *Los Angeles Times*, October 9, 1993, p. B2 (Orange County edition).

Not only did the media dutifully report the government schools' inventive claims, they joined the bandwagon with editorial broadsides of their own. The *Los Angeles Times* editorialized against the initiative three weeks in a row, on October 16, October 23, and October 30. The final editorial called Proposition 174 "a half-baked formula for beginning, in effect, the privatization of public schools by offering parents vouchers for private schools." In case readers missed the point, the editorial added, "Proposition 174 should get your 'no' vote, of course." The peroration: "Voting against 174 is a statement that one is not prepared to dismantle public schools."[26]

Union Opposition

Opposition from the schools and the mainstream media paled in comparison to that from the government school unions, particularly the CTA. ExCEL's statewide campaign payroll rarely exceeded a dozen people. The CTA had 12 staff members working full time against the initiative in Orange County alone, not to mention thousands of volunteers.[27] The anti-174 campaign never needed to create a grassroots organization or establish local or regional campaign headquarters; it simply worked through the CTA's existing structure.

The CTA provided full-time staff, an army of volunteers, and an established statewide organization. It also provided an amazing amount of money. By the week before the election, the CTA alone had spent $12.3 million to defeat Proposition 174.[28] The day before the election, the *Los Angeles Times* reported total spending on television commercials: proponents, $550,000; opponents, $6 million.

> Television ads by opponents started airing in September. The average voter 35 years and older sees one of the commercials eight times a week, their research shows. The messages went unanswered until 10 days ago when the proponents aired their first commercials. But the pro-174 campaign had

[26]"Voucher Initiative: What Will It Cost?" editorial, *Los Angeles Times*, October 16, 1993, P. B15 (Orange County edition); "Can't Vouch for Proposition 174," editorial, *Los Angeles Times*, October 23, 1993, p. B15 (Orange County edition); "Helping Schools — and Not Helping," editorial, *Los Angeles Times*, October 30, 1993, p. B15 (Orange County edition).

[27]Wilgoren, p. B1.

[28]"The Voucher Initiative: Savior or a Fatal Blow?" *Los Angeles Times*, October 31, 1993, p. A3.

enough money only for television spots in Southern and Central California; none aired in the Bay Area.[29]

Two months of virtually unanswered negative advertising had its effect. The race turned from a statistical dead heat into a rout:

> California voters have turned sharply and solidly against Proposition 174, the school voucher initiative, in the last month under the assault of a $6-million advertising campaign by opponents, the Los Angeles Times Poll has found.
>
> Two weeks before the Nov. 2 special statewide election, the voucher proposal trailed among registered voters by 59% to 26%. Those who said they were likely to vote opposed the measure by an even greater margin, 66% to 27%.
>
> Patricia Bullock, 68, of San Clemente summed up the feelings of the majority.
>
> "I do think we need to look at our educational system and crank it up, but . . . I believe [Proposition 174] would just destroy our public education system," said Bullock. . . .
>
> Proposition 174, the school voucher plan, was trailing in every major demographic group, including those thought to be its natural constituency—registered Republicans and conservatives. The only group that favored Proposition 174 was parents of children who are already in private schools—about 5% of the total sample.[30]

Table 8.1 gives voters' reasons for supporting or opposing Proposition 174.

The precipitous drop in popular support for Proposition 174 was credited to the CTA, which earned grudging respect for its heavy-handed but effective campaign:

> In the battle over the school vouchers initiative, the California Teachers Assn., which represents 230,000 public schoolteachers, has cemented its reputation as a free-spending special interest willing to use fierce campaign tactics.
>
> Pumped up by a multimillion-dollar campaign, the union could emerge from the vouchers fight as perhaps the most potent force in state politics.

[29]Dan Morain, "In Last-Ditch Effort, Prop. 174 Backers Go on Offensive," *Los Angeles Times*, November 1, 1993, pp. A3, A15.

[30]Bill Stall, "Opposition to School Vouchers Rises Sharply," *Los Angeles Times*, October 21, 1993, pp. A1, A33 (Orange County edition).

Table 8.1
Top Four Reasons for Support of or Opposition to Proposition 174, *Los Angeles Times* Poll Released October 21, 1993

What are you voting for Proposition 174?	
Allow parents greater choice	36%
Children will get better education	24%
Public schools aren't working	22%
Force public schools to compete	16%
Why are you voting against Proposition 174?	
Will destroy public schools	25%
Will drain needed money from public schools	19%
Allows unregulated schools with poor curriculum	19%
Gives tax money to private schools	13%

SOURCE: Bill Stall, "Opposition to School Vouchers Rises Sharply," analysis of poll, *Los Angeles Times,* October 21, 1993, p. A33 (Orange County edition).

NOTE: Up to two responses were accepted from each person surveyed.

"They've shown they can toss $10 million with the best of them," said Democratic fund-raiser Duane Garrett, one of the few Democrats who openly backs Proposition 174. "They are at the top of the charts in terms of an influential special interest."

The public campaign is being waged on the airwaves, where the coalition of public school unions is deluging voters with television and radio ads attacking Proposition 174.

But behind the scenes, the CTA-led coalition has displayed an extraordinary ability to dominate the campaign. . . .

The coalition fighting the initiative includes the 1-million-member California PTA, two teachers unions representing 270,000 teachers, and associations and unions representing administrators, school board members, bus drivers and other school employees.

In all, the groups have raised more than $16 million, with the CTA chipping in $12.3 million, making the fight over school vouchers one of California's costliest initiative campaigns. . . .

From the start of the campaign, in 1991 and early 1992, the public school unions made it clear that they would go to extremes to kill the initiative. In an early bulletin to teachers statewide, Weber called the voucher proposal "evil," and the CTA devised a strategy to stop it from reaching the ballot.[31]

The CTA's prominent role in the anti-174 juggernaut became a minor issue in itself. So pervasive and negative was CTA politicking that some voters had more doubts about the union itself than about the initiative it opposed:

> When you consider that the loudest opponents of school choice are the ones who stand to lose the most, you have to question their motives. By spending millions on deceptive radio and TV ads, it seems clear that the CTA and NEA are frantic about the threat to their power and position.[32]
>
> In the public school system, the union protects failing, has-been teachers and resists testing standards. In the union-free private system, you perform or you're out. Private schools have more direct accountability—to the parents. Try to have your public school remove a non-performing teacher and measure your success.[33]
>
> Neither parents nor the marketplace is flawless, but I'll trust them over the CTA bureaucracy any day.[34]

Sharing their opinion was former California governor George Deukmejian, one of Proposition 174's leading advocates. According to columnist George Skelton, Deukmejian considered the CTA "ungrateful, selfish and shortsighted":

> Deukmejian was considered an "education governor" early in his first term. He signed and funded a landmark reform bill—SB 813, the number rolls off his tongue. During his eight-year tenure, he increased school funding 115% while student enrollments rose only 23%. . . .
>
> "There were two defining incidents when I was governor that helped form my opinion," he explains. One occurred when he invited education leaders to his office to discuss prioritizing programs—spending more money on the best and eliminating the worst. "What they wanted was full funding for every existing program," he says. "They didn't want to talk—nothing."

[31]Dan Morain, "Teachers Union Flexes New Muscle in Leading Fight against Prop. 174," *Los Angeles Times*, October 25, 1993, p. A3 (Orange County edition).

[32]Jim Durbin, letter, *Los Angeles Times*, October 10, 1993, p. B15 (Orange County edition).

[33]David A. Frazer, letter, *Los Angeles Times*, October 10, 1993, p. B15 (Orange County edition).

[34]Cynthia L. Crowe, letter, *Los Angeles Times*, October 10, 1993, p. B15 (Orange County edition).

Then later, Deukmejian offered schools more money to reduce class sizes. The CTA objected, he says, because it wanted all the money to be used for teacher salaries.[35]

Profiles in Courage

The only statewide official willing to join Deukmejian in support of the initiative and in opposition to the CTA was attorney general Dan Lungren. Other political "leaders," state and federal, fell into line behind the CTA. Foremost among them was President Clinton. In a speech to the AFL-CIO convention in San Francisco on October 4, he urged Californians to defeat Proposition 174.[36] Despite finding public schools unacceptable for his own daughter, he apparently considered them adequate for ordinary citizens.

Although Proposition 174 had been the most hotly debated public policy proposal in the state for two full years, California governor Pete Wilson took no position on it until the political trends were clear. On October 5 he announced his opposition, claiming that the potential cost of awarding tuition vouchers to existing private school students could worsen the state's already serious budget imbalance. The *Los Angeles Times* noted:

> The governor announced his stand a day after President Clinton came out against Proposition 174 on the Nov. 2 ballot, and weeks after state Treasurer Kathleen Brown and Insurance Commissioner John Garamendi, Wilson's main Democratic rivals for the 1994 gubernatorial election, took their stands against it. . . .
>
> Wilson's stand appeared to push him further from conservatives in his party, including potential GOP presidential candidates.
>
> William J. Bennett, education secretary under President Ronald Reagan, and Jack Kemp, former housing and urban development secretary under President George Bush, have come out in favor of the initiative. Former Gov. George Deukmejian also supports the initiative, as does the California Republican Party.[37]

[35]George Skelton, "Prop. 174 Stirs Old Flames in Deukmejian," *Los Angeles Times,* October 11, 1993, p. A3 (Orange County edition).

[36]Lauter, p. A3.

[37]Dan Morain, "School Voucher Initiative Too Expensive, Wilson Says," *Los Angeles Times,* October 6, 1993, pp. A1, A18 (Orange County edition).

Winning honors for the crassest political performance was former representative Tom Campbell, a liberal Republican who lost the Republican primary for a U.S. Senate seat to conservative Bruce Herschensohn in 1992. During that campaign one of the very few issues upon which Herschensohn and Campbell agreed was school choice; both endorsed Proposition 174 without reservation. In 1993 Campbell decided to run for a state senate seat in Silicon Valley. Campbell began the race not only as a proponent of 174, but as a fundraiser for it. The *Los Angeles Times* explains what happened next.

> Realizing that Campbell would be running a campaign that included a pro-voucher stand, former CTA President Ed Foglia declared that he would run against Campbell.
>
> [Current CTA president Del] Weber, a former Anaheim High School mathematics teacher, told reporters that the CTA not only would support Foglia, "we would saturate that area" with money and campaign workers. . . .
>
> Campbell made an about-face, announcing that after reading the measure more closely, he opposed it. The CTA disarmed, and Foglia dropped out.[38]

One has to feel pity for a candidate so utterly incapable of saving face. Nobody believed that Campbell's flip-flop was motivated by genuine concerns about the initiative's effect. A former Stanford law professor, Campbell could hardly claim to have been misled or confused by the initiative's legal language or to have missed something in his reading of the text. The only plausible explanation is the obvious one: the CTA was not a factor in Campbell's U.S. Senate primary, but it was a major factor in his state senate race. He responded accordingly.

Results

The opponents of Proposition 174 completely dominated the campaign. They set the agenda, defined the themes, and drove their message home through relentless repetition. So effective were they that the abysmal performance of public schools was hardly mentioned in the closing weeks of the campaign. Proponents had intended to make the election a referendum on public school performance, with which the public was overwhelmingly dissatisfied, and parental choice, which the public overwhelmingly wanted. Instead,

[38]Morain, "Teachers Union Flexes New Muscle," p. A3.

they found themselves on the defensive against charges that the initiative would raise taxes and weaken the government schools only to fund new schools set up by charlatans and fanatics.

The nature of the campaign's concluding weeks is typified by this excerpt of an interview with Joe Alibrandi, chairman of ExCEL:

> Q: There's nothing in this initiative to stop any so-called religion or cult from opening a tax-supported voucher school. Would you really want your tax money to go to a People's Temple school?
>
> ALIBRANDI: We have millions of kids incarcerated in inner-city schools all up and down the state of California who are being cheated out of an education. Who's worrying about them? You talk about witches' schools. Some of these schools are worse than that. The kids are not getting an education. They are being pushed in the direction of being an underclass. Their safety is jeopardized. That is the reality.[39]

Alibrandi made sense, but not headlines. The allegations were all over the airwaves; the answers were in occasional newspaper interviews.

On November 2, 1993, Californians went to the polls. Proposition 174 lost in all 58 counties. There were 1,561,514 votes (30.44 percent) in favor and 3,567,834 (69.56 percent) opposed.[40]

[39]"The Voucher Initiative," pp. A3, A35.
[40]California Secretary of State.

9. Postmortem

"The Case for Vouchers Has Barely Been Heard"

Although Proposition 174 was defeated by a margin of more than two to one, news reports and commentaries emphasized not the magnitude of the loss but the disparity in campaign resources. The *Los Angeles Times* reported that

> the results reflected the lopsided money war: Voucher proponents were outspent by more than 4 to 1. Opponents raked in more than $17 million to defeat Proposition 174. Proponents raised $4.1 million, much of it in 1991 and early 1992 to get the measure on the ballot. That left them with about $2.5 million to mount their campaign. . . .
>
> At the start of the drive this summer, [Yes on 174 strategist Ken] Khachigian said his campaign had a budget of $5 million to $6 million. He ended up trying to organize a campaign and buy television time on only $2.5 million.
>
> "Their attempt to get the large businesses and the prestige businesses to support the initiative failed totally," said [Stanford University professor Michael] Kirst. "The business community just took a walk on this initiative and that obviously hurt them fiscally."
>
> Proposition 174 had been scheduled to appear on the June, 1994, ballot. But when Gov. Wilson convened Tuesday's special election to decide the fate of his half-cent sales tax surcharge, the voucher initiative automatically went onto the November ballot, catching proponents by surprise. They had almost no money or organization.
>
> "We were planning our fundraising and political organization for 1994, not 1993," said Sam Hardage, a San Diego hotel operator and fund-raiser for Proposition 174. "We had to create an entire campaign in just a few weeks."
>
> The opponents, by contrast, had a war chest filled by assessments from the paychecks of nearly every public school teacher and employee, plus an organization of more than

1,000 union field representatives across the state. Public
employee unions provided $16 million—$12.5 million of
which came from the California Teachers Assn.[1]

The opposition's $17 million campaign bought a landslide only
because proponents' $2.5 million was insufficient to buy a retaining
wall. Thus, who *didn't* spend is as significant as who did. As David
Broder writes:

> In California, the case for vouchers has barely been heard,
> because the people who pay for conservative campaigns have
> not anted up for this one. Why not? In the blunt words of
> Ken Khachigian, the veteran conservative strategist who runs
> the campaign, "Business wimped out."
>
> "They are too far removed from the tragedy of our bad
> public schools," Khachigian said. "Their kids are already
> in private schools or going to Beverly Hills High or Palos
> Verdes High. . . ."
>
> The fact is that the same people who would finance candi-
> dates against Pat Brown and Tom Bradley, against Jimmy
> Carter and Walter Mondale, the people who paid for initia-
> tives that would reduce their taxes and guarantee shortened
> tenure for their enemies in the Legislature and Congress,
> would not come through with big bucks for a voucher pro-
> gram proponents say would be of biggest benefit to the mid-
> dle class and poor.
>
> That says something significant—and shameful—about
> the condition of conservatism in this country.[2]

Whatever the reason, proponents of Proposition 174 were unable
to raise the money needed to run a competitive race. Opponents
saturated the airwaves with virtually unanswered negative advertising. The lopsided results reflected the lopsided campaign budgets.
The voters never rejected Proposition 174; they never learned what
it was. Instead they rejected a ridiculous caricature of it conjured
up by those with the most to lose from its passage.

"Smugness Will Not Be Warranted"

With little money left in the Yes on 174 treasury and polls predict-
ing a two to one defeat, postmortems began appearing well before

[1]Dan Morain and Jodi Wilgoren, "State Voters Reject School Vouchers 2-1," *Los
Angeles Times,* November 3, 1993, pp. A1, A26, A27.

[2]David S. Broder, "Shameful Silence on School Vouchers," *Washington Post,*
October 27, 1993.

election day. But no one considered Proposition 174's impending defeat a victory for the status quo. The campaign did nothing to dissipate pervasive dissatisfaction with the dismal performance of government schools. George Skelton warns the education establishment that

> any sense of euphoria or smugness will not be warranted. In most voters' minds, this election is not a referendum on public schools, despite the attempt of voucher advocates to turn it into that. If it were, Proposition 174 would win by a landslide.
>
> Voters who oppose the measure do so mainly because they fear it would destroy public schools by draining off needed tax dollars, The Times Poll found. They also don't like the idea of public funds going to unregulated private schools.
>
> But only 4% of those who reject Proposition 174 actually like the current public school system. And just 1% feel that new school reforms are adequate. Similarly, the Field Poll found that only 5% of the measure's opponents believe "public schools are doing the best they can." And just 3% think "things are OK the way they are...."
>
> If the pollsters are right, public schools will be given another chance. It may be their last.[3]

Many parents fear that government schools are failing to provide a safe and disciplined learning environment for their children— or, for that matter, to provide much learning at all. The education establishment dismisses these serious and justified fears as "racist or anti-public school," observes Adela de la Torre, even though "Mexican-American and African-American parents" are especially subject to them. She writes:

> To ignore the roots of why Proposition 174 is on the ballot and not engage in an honest debate of why it crosses racial, ethnic and class lines is to lose an opportunity to assess the shortcomings of our system and create an alternative vision of public education for our children. Despite its limitations, Proposition 174 speaks to real fears of parents that must be addressed by public education. Be assured that these fears will not dissipate after November's election.[4]

[3]George Skelton, "Even If It Fails, Prop. 174 Is a Wake-Up Call," *Los Angeles Times*, November 1, 1993, p. A3.

[4]Adela de la Torre, "Voucher Opponents Miss the Point," *Los Angeles Times*, October 20, 1993, p. B9 (Orange County edition).

De la Torre was right: those fears did not dissipate. Government school approval ratings remain in the cellar. Voters are deeply dissatisfied with the government school system, and they have no faith that the cosmetic reforms offered as alternatives to school choice will produce meaningful change. Opponents of school choice never persuaded the public that the government schools were doing well, only that Proposition 174 was flawed. They claimed that Proposition 174 would raise taxes, fund unqualified or extremist schools, and further weaken the already underperforming government schools. Proposition 174's defeat reflects those concerns—not contentment with the status quo.

"Too Great a Gamble"

Most commentators attributed Proposition 174's defeat principally to the disparity in campaign funding. A few, however, placed at least partial blame on the text of the initiative itself. Their principal concerns were fiscal and regulatory. "Voters across the state concluded that Proposition 174 was simply too great a gamble," reported the *Los Angeles Times*, "both with the state's pocketbook and with California's 5.2 million public school children."[5]

Fiscal Impact

Too great a gamble? This conclusion illustrates a frequent frustration of 174's proponents: those who attacked the initiative for potentially allowing hypothetical and highly improbable risks blithely ignored the definite dangers of maintaining the status quo. As Stephen J. Carroll of the RAND Corporation explains,

> voting against 174 is also a gamble. We face a looming fiscal crisis. Spending on K–12 education already consumes almost one-third of California's entire general-fund revenues. Our projections show that by the years 2002–2003, this share will rise to 43%. That's even bigger than it sounds, because a large part of state spending is locked into entitlements. As the number of pupils continues to grow, something will have to change in the state's public-finance system.[6]

[5]Morain and Wilgoren, p. A26.

[6]Stephen J. Carroll, "Rolling the Dice with Prop. 174," *Los Angeles Times*, October 5, 1993, p. B11 (Orange County edition).

The defeat of 174 would present "three unpalatable options," Carroll concludes: (1) slash per-student spending on the government schools, (2) cut other state services, or (3) raise taxes.

Proposition 174 offered a better choice: it would have enabled the private sector to help accommodate California's burgeoning enrollment at half the government school system's per-student cost. Rather than raising taxes to continue providing a high-cost, low-result education to almost all students through the government school system, 174 would have enabled independent schools to welcome as many children as they wanted. The long-term fiscal implications are obvious: the more tuition vouchers the state issues, the more the taxpayers save.

So what was the alleged fiscal fear? Opponents argued that Proposition 174 would cost the taxpayers over a billion dollars a year. The argument is fallacious, but the *Wall Street Journal's* Albert Hunt accepts it uncritically:

> Voters became aware there was a price tag; it would cost more than a billion dollars just to give the existing 10% of California schoolchildren who are in private schools a $2,600 voucher. Moreover, to make school choice economically feasible, experts estimated that 20% more of California's 5.7 million schoolkids would have to opt for private-school vouchers, yet that would require about 2,000 new schools.[7]

Mr. Hunt is repeating the claim that if every one of California's half-million independent school students used a $2,600 scholarship voucher, and no government school students did so, school choice would cost the state $1.3 billion in the first year. That is tantamount to saying that if my aunt were a man, she would be my uncle. The conclusion follows from the premises, but the premises do not describe reality.

Had Mr. Hunt read the initiative, he would have learned the following:

First, students already enrolled in independent schools do not qualify for the scholarships for two years. Government school students, in contrast, qualify immediately. Every government school student who accepts a scholarship costs the taxpayers $2,600 instead

[7]Albert R. Hunt, "A Day of Defeat for Democrats," *Wall Street Journal*, November 4, 1993, p. A15.

of $5,200. Thus the state accumulates substantial savings for two years before incurring any new costs from phasing in existing independent school students.

Second, no school with fewer than 25 students may redeem scholarships. That provision excludes not only home schools but a significant number of small independent schools. So, yes, assuming there were no offsetting savings, it would cost more than a billion dollars to give the scholarships to all existing independent school students— but the initiative does not do that.

Third, no school may be compelled to accept scholarships, and during the campaign some schools announced that they in fact would not. Their reasons vary. Some expensive college preparatory academies have no need of scholarships; they have waiting lists of wealthy students already. Some church-sponsored institutions, despite 174's careful efforts to protect them from increased regulation, fear that by accepting the scholarships they will lose their independence. They especially fear state interference with their curriculum. Whatever their reasons, some otherwise eligible schools will choose not to participate in the scholarship program.

Of California's half-million independent school students, over 100,000 are in home schools or other schools with fewer than 25 students. Of the remaining 400,000, perhaps 50,000 attend schools that will opt out of the scholarship program. Another group of students will graduate from or transfer out of the independent schools during the two-year phase-in period. Thus, the actual number of existing independent school students accepting scholarships will probably be closer to 300,000 than 500,000.

Every existing independent school student who uses a scholarship costs the taxpayers $2,600. But every government school student who uses a scholarship *saves* the taxpayers $2,600. Accordingly, if the number of government school students using the scholarships to transfer to independent schools matches the number of existing independent school students using the scholarships to stay where they are, the program involves no net cost. And every additional transfer to independent schools saves even more tax money.

During the two-year phase-in period, can the independent schools handle 300,000 new students transferring from the government schools? Almost certainly. That is only 150,000 students per year—not far beyond the independent school system's existing excess capacity.

In all probability Proposition 174 would save tax money in every year of its operation. A fiscal-impact analysis prepared by the Bionomics Institute, assuming a relatively modest 10 percent annual transfer rate, predicts that within 10 years government schools and independent schools will each have about 50 percent market share. Under those conditions, the initiative

will reduce total state and local K–12 education expenditures by approximately $59 billion during its first ten fiscal years. . . . The annual savings to taxpayers will rise from $1.5 billion in the program's first year (1994/5) up to $10.4 billion, or $821 per household in its tenth year (2003/4).

These savings will be generated as students transfer from conventional public schools—where each student costs taxpayers $5367 per year—to scholarship schools, where each student will cost taxpayers 50% of that amount, or $2684 per scholarship. As the population of transferred students accumulates, the share of California's K–12 student population attending conventional public schools will decline. . . . Annual savings to taxpayers will increase as this shift progresses. . . .

Between 1994/5 and 2003/4, an influx of 2.1 million additional students will join the existing K–12 public and private enrollment of 6.2 million, raising the total student population to 8.3 million. According to Department of Education projections, without [Proposition 174] this influx of new students to the conventional public school population would require as much as $20 billion in new school construction. . . .

We have not attempted to estimate the additional savings generated as the student population shifts into facilities not financed by taxpayers. Consequently, the savings projected here significantly understate the actual savings that would be generated. . . .

This Amendment could fail to generate savings in state and local K–12 expenditures only if the net transfer rate stayed under 1.75%. Only under this unrealistically low (one in sixty students) transfer rate are the savings generated by transfer from conventional public to scholarship schools insufficient to offset the cost of scholarships for students currently enrolled in conventional private schools.[8]

[8]Bionomics Institute, *Fiscal Impact Analysis of the California Parental Choice Scholarship Amendment,* Summary Report (San Rafael, Calif.: Bionomics Institute, June 30, 1993), pp. 1–3.

The Excellence through Choice in Education League's own fiscal-impact analysis reached similar conclusions, projecting annual savings increasing from $1.2 billion in the program's first year of operation to $7.6 billion in the eighth year.[9] The ExCEL analysis reports on current excess capacity and future expansion plans of California's independent schools and concludes that capacity constraints will not hinder the tuition scholarship program. A well-known historical precedent indicates that private school supply is quite elastic:

> The Servicemen's Readjustment Act of 1944, commonly referred to as the "G.I. Bill," provided reimbursement for tuition and other college expenses for returning World War II veterans.
> Appendix 4 lists enrollment figures in public and private colleges immediately before and after the enactment of the G.I. Bill. These figures provide a startling example of how quickly the private sector in education can respond to a surge in demand for its services.
> In 1939 private college enrollment stood at 638,250. In the middle of World War II during 1943–1944, enrollment was 583,866. During 1945–1946, enrollment surged to 849,048. This is a 33% increase over pre-war enrollment levels and a 45% increase over the [enrollment of two years earlier].[10]

This dramatic enrollment growth is especially striking in light of the high educational requirements for college faculty. K–12 expansion should be no more difficult.

In summary, fiscal concerns are an argument for the initiative, not against it. The government school system can accommodate California's increasing enrollment only at tremendous cost. The initiative enables the private sector to accommodate a growing number of students at substantial savings.

Extremist Schools

"But what are taxpayers going to think about footing the bill for Islamic fundamentalist schools or black Muslim institutions, or religious-right home-schooling practitioners?" asks Albert Hunt.[11]

[9]David Barulich, *Fiscal Impact Analysis of the Parental Choice in Education Amendment,* presented to the Legislative Analyst Office, California state legislature, June 23, 1992; Appendix 23.

[10]Ibid., p. 7.

[11]Hunt, p. A15.

Again, had Mr. Hunt bothered to read the initiative, he could have saved his ink. To review:

Paragraph (b)(2) excludes any school that advocates unlawful behavior or teaches hatred of any person or group on the basis of race, national origin, religion, or gender. If an Islamic fundamentalist school, or any other school, violates those standards it cannot redeem scholarships. If the school complies, on the other hand, who cares what God its students pray to?

Paragraph (b)(1) excludes any school that discriminates on the basis of race. If a Black Muslim institution restricted admission to blacks, it could not qualify to redeem scholarships.

Subsection (b)(3) excludes home schools.

It may be true that voters were concerned about Proposition 174's fiscal impact or the prospect of extremist or unqualified schools. Those concerns, however, arose from the campaign against the initiative, not from the text of the initiative itself. Commentators who recommend addressing these concerns in future proposals generally fail to realize that the initiative already does so. While improvements and refinements in the text are certainly possible—in fact, Chapter 11 recommends some—proponents cannot expect textual changes alone to inoculate future proposals against negative campaigning.

"Republican Voters Didn't Want It"

Another school of thought holds that Proposition 174 lost not because of the opposition campaign or assumed flaws in the text, but because mainstream suburban voters perceive school choice as more of a threat than an opportunity. Some suburban parents have moved into pricey areas specifically to take advantage of relatively good government schools. Others have invested considerable time in their schools by volunteering as room mothers, serving as aides, participating in the parent-teacher association, and so on. These parents may perceive *other* government schools as mediocre, but they consider *their* government school superior. Some of these parents fear that school choice will weaken their local schools, to which they are loyal. John Miller argues that these are the voters who defeated 174:

> School choice boosters have already started rattling off
> dozens of reasons for the failure: They were wildly outspent
> by powerful special interests, activist teachers turned their

155

classrooms into anti-choice workshops, the media tarred supporters as religious fanatics, etc. All of these claims are to some extent true. But each misses the big picture: School choice failed in California because Republican voters didn't want it. . . .

Most suburbanites—the folks who make up the GOP's rank-and-file—are happy with their kids' school systems. Their children already earn good grades, score well on tests, and gain admission into reputable colleges and universities. . . .

In [a recent poll], only 19% of suburbia awarded grades of A or B to the nation's public schools, but 50% gave an A or B to the public schools in their communities. The last thing these satisfied parents want is an education revolution. . . .

School choicers clearly have to lobby the suburbs, where their lack of support currently dooms them.

To do this, they should stop lecturing the suburbs about lousy schools. For starters, the suburbanites aren't likely to believe it. More important, they view the charge as defamation. Since they often take an active role in their children's education, arguing that their schools are bad is tantamount to calling them crummy parents. It's a slap in the face and it won't ever win votes.

Instead, school choicers will have to make pocketbook appeals. Success in the suburbs will require emphasis on the financial savings that a good school choice plan will deliver.[12]

Miller's diagnosis is better than his prescription. He is correct in arguing that proponents need to do a better job of persuading suburban voters. Pocketbook appeals may be a part of that effort; indeed, they were a part of the campaign for Proposition 174, which every major taxpayer organization in California endorsed. But ExCEL's polling showed that promises of reduced spending on education did not appeal to most voters, who tend to equate increased spending with greater commitment and better performance. Reduced spending may be a beneficial result of school choice, but it is not a strong selling point. Pocketbook appeals will work only if they are linked to quality appeals. "Spending less on education" is a sure loser at the ballot box. "Allowing independent schools to do a better job at a lower cost" may become a winner.

[12]John J. Miller, "Why School Choice Lost," *Wall Street Journal*, November 4, 1993, p. A14.

Miller apparently wants to ignore the quality question, however; he tells proponents to "stop lecturing the suburbs about lousy schools." But if the schools are okay, why should the taxpayers fund alternatives to them? The fact is that even relatively good suburban schools are doing an inadequate job of preparing students for the demands and opportunities of the 21st century. School choice may be needed most urgently by students in poor inner-city schools, but students in prosperous suburbs will benefit as well.

Miller adds that the school choice movement should change its vocabulary. " 'Scholarship,' he writes, "sounds so much more appealing than 'voucher.' "[13] Miller neglects to credit Proposition 174 for having already done precisely what he recommends. The word "voucher" never appears in the text of Proposition 174; the word "scholarship" appears instead. The Yes on 174 campaign almost always employed the same term.

Nobel laureate Gary Becker puts a different spin on the fiscal argument. "The vouchers should be provided only to low-income families," he writes; that would avoid most of the fiscal impact of including existing independent school students.[14] But exit polls clearly indicate that voters do not want tuition vouchers based on financial need.[15] Moreover, if finances are the concern we ought to include more students, not fewer, since the proposed scholarship amount is only 50 percent of the per-pupil government school cost.

"A Vastly Different Approach Must Be Taken"

Opponents of school choice did not have a superior proposal; they merely had superior funding. School choice was defeated not because of flaws in the concept or text of Proposition 174, but because of inadequate coalition building and fundraising. The good news: with a broader supporting coalition and a deeper treasury, future school choice efforts can succeed. The challenge: government school-teachers, administrators, and other employees will always fight to maintain their protected positions in the current system. They will convert their unions, and the government school system itself, into a

[13]Ibid.

[14]Gary S. Becker, "School-Finance Reform: Don't Give Up on Vouchers," *Business Week*, December 27, 1993, p. 25.

[15]Stephanie Chavez and Dan Morain, "Voucher Backers Vow to Continue Fight," *Los Angeles Times*, November 4, 1993, pp. A3, A37.

statewide campaign organization and fundraising mechanism. Well-organized, amply funded, and with an obvious self-interest in keeping the status quo, such opposition will not easily be overcome. As the *Los Angeles Times* notes:

> After sound defeats of similar voucher initiatives in Oregon and Colorado, the heavy California loss indicates that a vastly different approach must be taken to overcome the powerful education Establishment and its employee unions, which pumped nearly limitless resources into campaigns to defeat the measures.[16]

What should that different approach be? For some ideas, let's consider the success of a few less-ambitious school choice programs.

[16]Ibid.

PART III

FUTURE PROSPECTS

10. Why Choice Works

Although statewide school choice initiatives were defeated in Oregon in 1990, Colorado in 1992, and California in 1993, more modest school choice programs are operating elsewhere. The state of Wisconsin offers a limited number of tuition vouchers to low-income students in Milwaukee. Some states and school districts allow choice among government schools. Most promising of all, privately funded tuition voucher programs are operating in several cities. School choice in any form proves popular wherever it is tried.

Milwaukee, Wisconsin

Polly Williams is the Rosa Parks of school choice. As a state representative in the Wisconsin legislature, she led the effort to offer independent school scholarships to inner-city Milwaukee students. In the wake of her success, she has become America's leading advocate of parental choice in education. Here is her story, in her own words:

> For what amounts to a 90 percent failure rate, we pay $600 million a year to support the Milwaukee public schools—that averages out to about $6000 per student. The educrats keep saying, "You've got to give us more money, because it's tough to educate these inner city kids. They are poor, and they are raised by single mothers; we can't expect them to learn."
>
> That's the stereotype: poor black children are slow learners, difficult and expensive to educate. Well, my children were raised in a single parent home. My husband and I divorced when the eldest was thirteen and the youngest was five. After the divorce, five of us had to live on my salary, which was only $8000 a year. And we did live on it, though we were certainly living below the poverty level. According to the educrats and all the experts defining who we were, my children *were simply not supposed to make it.* I am happy

to tell you that the educrats were wrong, because my children *did* make it and they are not stereotypes.

But poor black children *do* share a major disadvantage. Unlike those whose parents can vote with their feet and enroll in good private schools, poor black children are forced to go to the school the government selects for them. That's not right. We're supposed to educate *all* children, because if we don't educate them we're going to incarcerate them. . . . Blacks want to learn and earn their way just like everybody else. We don't want welfare that just puts us back on the plantation.

Representative Williams explains that a dozen independent schools in inner Milwaukee provided "a wonderful alternative" for minority students, with "teachers who really believed in *them*, rather than the educrats' stereotypes." They graduated fully 98 percent of their students (compared to 40 percent in the government schools).

But they couldn't get by on the tuition they charged, and although successful, they were in danger of closing their doors. Meanwhile, the public schools were getting millions of our tax dollars whether they did a good job or not. So a few years ago, a small group banded together and approached the state legislature. We said: "Why not allow tax dollars to go to the schools that *are* working?" We didn't know that vouchers had already been defeated in every other state where they'd been proposed. We didn't even call our proposal a voucher plan; we called it "parental empowerment" or "choice." Meetings were organized to discuss our proposal. We hoped to attract a few dozen people, but hundreds of enthusiastic parents began showing up and staying for sessions that ran on for hours. This shocked public school officials, especially since they couldn't get more than a few parents to any of *their* meetings.

Naturally, the education establishment opposed Polly's plan. The teachers unions and the bureaucrats associations were far too powerful to beat on their own turf, so Polly Williams and her allies went around them, organizing hundreds of parents into a grassroots political force. Soon poor parents were observing the legislature from the capitol galleries. The result?

To everyone's surprise, the parental empowerment bill—the first in the U.S.—passed into law. Starting in the 1990–91 school year, up to 1000 students could claim $2500 worth of tuition vouchers (a fraction, of course, of the per-student expense at public schools). This year, one private school had 600 applicants for 100 openings. Every private school in the inner city has a waiting list. Hundreds of low-income families want out of the public school system. Those who have succeeded in getting out are spreading the word: Their children, two to three grade levels behind in the public school, are now working at their grade levels. Once always absent, they are even refusing to stay home sick.[1]

With strong support from Wisconsin governor Tommy Thompson, a conservative Republican, state representative Polly Williams, a liberal Democrat, had managed to push the parental empowerment–school choice bill through the legislature. With strong support from parents, the program had begun working. A new coalition was developing, including Republicans and Democrats, whites and blacks, suburban and urban voters. A poll of Wisconsin residents found that 59 percent of them supported the Milwaukee school choice program; among blacks, the figure was a politically unheard of 83 percent.[2] The *New York Times* reported that "as the program's first semester draws to a close, the parents speak in jubilant tones about their children's progress, directors of the six participating private schools describe a relatively smooth transition and Javon Williams, for one, says that for the first time he looks forward to school."[3]

Virtually all participants in the Milwaukee program are minority students; 59 percent of participating families receive public assistance, and 76 percent are headed by single parents. A study commissioned by the Wisconsin legislature recommended that the program be continued. Among its findings: "Rather than skimming off the best students, this program seems to provide an alternative educational environment for students who are not doing particularly well in the public school system."[4]

[1] A. Polly Williams, "Inner City Kids: Why Choice Is Their Only Hope," *Imprimis*, March 1992, pp. 2–4; emphasis in original.

[2] "Choice Facts," editorial, *Wall Street Journal*, February 6, 1992.

[3] Isabel Wilkerson, "For 345, Poverty Is Key to Door of Private School," *New York Times*, December 19, 1990.

[4] John F. Witte, *First Year Report: Milwaukee Parental Choice Program* (Madison: Robert M. LaFollette Institute of Public Affairs, University of Wisconsin, 1991), Executive Summary, p. iv.

It seemed that everyone liked the program—everyone, that is, except the Wisconsin Association of School District Administrators, the Wisconsin Education Association Council, the Association of Wisconsin School Administrators, the Milwaukee Teachers Education Association, the Milwaukee Administrators & Supervisors Council, the Wisconsin Federation of Teachers, and Superintendent of Public Instruction Herb Grover. These representatives of the education establishment threw their combined weight and their massive budgets into a series of legal challenges designed to overturn, or at least thwart, the parental empowerment–school choice program. Who defended the program? A handful of the inner-city mothers it was helping, along with a few of the thinly funded inner-city independent schools their children were finally able to attend. It was David and Goliath all over again, both in the mismatched size of the combatants and, fortunately, in the outcome. On March 3, 1992, the Wisconsin Supreme Court upheld the parental empowerment–school choice program in every particular.[5] In his opinion concurring with the majority, Justice Louis J. Ceci wrote:

> Let's give choice a chance!
> Literally thousands of school children in the Milwaukee public school system have been doomed because of those in government who insist upon maintaining the status quo. . . .
> The Wisconsin legislature, attuned . . . to the appalling and seemingly insurmountable problems confronting socioeconomically deprived children, has attempted to throw a life preserver to those Milwaukee children caught in the cruel riptide of a school system floundering upon the shoals of poverty, status quo thinking, and despair.
> The dissent by Justice Bablitch attempts to paint a difference in that the schools that these deprived children would attend under this experimental program would be the recipients of "the state's largesse." IMAGINE THAT! If the expenditure of a mere $2,500.00 per child to teach the deprived children of the poor of the city of Milwaukee is—largesse—what foolishness are we engaged in when the taxpayers are spending approximately $5,000.00 for each of these same children in a failing public school system?[6]

[5]*Davis* v. *Grover*, 166 Wis. 2d 501, 480 N.W. 2d 460 (1992).

[6]*Davis* v. *Grover*, Wisconsin Supreme Court opinion no. 90–1807, filed March 3, 1992; slip opinion, concurring opinion at 2; capitalization is in the original.

The education establishment fought the Milwaukee choice program every step of the way, but the parents and students won. "Polly Williams and the hundreds of kids she has helped . . . can finally relax," reported the *Wall Street Journal*. "The parents involved are highly pleased."[7] "The Milwaukee program scores well in parent satisfaction," agrees the *Los Angeles Times*:

> Milwaukee parents who have used the program praise the private schools for providing safe environments for children to learn, more individualized attention from teachers and tighter discipline. . . .
>
> Gloria Collins enrolled her daughter, Natasha, in Urban Day four years ago because Natasha, then a third-grader, could not read or do simple arithmetic and had to be forced to go to school. Now, in the sixth grade, she is earning a steady C average.
>
> More important to Collins, a dropout who got her high school equivalency degree and works as a teacher's assistant at Urban Day, Natasha is happy about going to school each morning. Collins says her daughter's positive attitude is all the proof she needs that choice is a success.
>
> "In public schools if you don't have it, they won't work with you to get it," she said. "They let you ride along until you get fed up with riding and you drop out."
>
> Every parent is expected to be involved in the school. Urban Day's motto this year is: "It takes a whole village to raise a child." Discipline is tough, but the atmosphere is warm. . . .
>
> In classroom after classroom in the impeccably clean, colorfully decorated school, students are well behaved and engaged in their work. The test results do not reflect it yet, but [Urban Day School principal Robb] Rauh believes they soon will show the school is having a positive impact on students' academic abilities.[8]

What do parents find in the independent schools that they cannot find in their government schools? Small classes, a safe and clean learning environment, and caring but demanding teachers.

---

[7]"Polly's Victory," editorial, *Wall Street Journal*, March 10, 1992.

[8]Elizabeth Shogren, "A Chance to See Choice at Work," *Los Angeles Times*, October 22, 1993, pp. A1, A16.

"I never had a teacher that I felt cared about me and wanted to help me until I came to Harambee [another independent school in the Milwaukee program]," said fourth-grader Ethan Hill, dressed in one of Harambee's forest green-and-white uniforms.

"Too many eighth-graders were picking on me because I got good grades," Elton Gofoe, 9, added. "Here, good grades are cool."

Ruthie Brown, Harambee's full-time disciplinarian, says choice provides a glimmer of hope for the children who live in its rough, gang-run neighborhood, where drive-by shootings and drugs are part of daily life. . . .

"I'm doing this to save our children," said Brown, who lives in the neighborhood and has sent her children to Harambee. "We've got a lost generation out there, and we're going to lose another one unless we help them develop self-discipline and self-esteem and provide a safe place for them to learn."[9]

Indianapolis, Indiana

Supporters of parental choice around the nation have tried to accomplish what Polly Williams did, but they cannot seem to get school choice bills out of their state legislatures. J. Patrick Rooney, chairman of the Golden Rule Insurance Company, decided that waiting for government action meant "abandoning another generation of children who are not getting a decent education." Rather than let that happen, his company created a privately funded school choice program. Without any state participation, the Golden Rule Insurance Company offered to pay half tuition, up to an $800 cap, for any low-income student wanting to attend an independent school. Mr. Rooney tells what happened next:

We called a press conference to announce the start of the program only three weeks before the commencement of the 1991–92 school year. We stated very cautiously that we anticipated that only 100–200 students would want to be involved in this program. Well, within the first three days, Golden Rule had 621 requests for applications, and at the present time [October 1991], we have distributed more than 2,000 applications.

[9]Ibid.

A temporary obstacle is that most of the private schools already have full or near-full enrollments. But the response to our private voucher plan will inevitably lead to expansion, as it has created a whole new supply of potential students for private schools. In the first school term of this year, 705 students were awarded vouchers and there were 199 on the waiting list. (This list would have been larger, but many parents knew that the private schools were full.)[10]

Other business leaders joined Mr. Rooney in supporting the plan, and in the 1992–93 school year, the CHOICE Charitable Trust awarded scholarship vouchers to 944 students.[11]

Each of those students comes from a family that could not otherwise afford independent school. Patricia Farnan describes "the superhuman effort of parents working two or three jobs, cutting corners at home to manage their meager budgets, doing whatever possible to give their children the gift made possible by the CHOICE voucher."[12] What motivates parents to make such a sacrifice? In answer, Farnan quotes Rev. Charles Barcus, principal of Calvary Christian School:

> "A typical child who transfers from the public school to Calvary Christian has grown so fearful of physical harm and other threatening conditions that he has literally shut down his desire to learn. Parents come to me desperate to put their child back on an academic track. In many cases the risks are high, for the students are literally failing out of the public school. Nothing could be more rewarding than watching them blossom again into happy children with a strong curiosity to learn."[13]

The experience Reverend Barcus described is all too common. Parents want their children to learn, they want them to understand basic values, and above all they want them to be safe. For low-income parents, the vouchers make that possible.

---

[10]J. Patrick Rooney, "Private Vouchers: A New Idea in Education Reform," *Imprimis*, March 1992, pp. 1, 4.

[11]Patricia Farnan, "A Choice for Etta Wallace," *Policy Review*, Spring 1993, p. 24.

[12]Ibid., p. 25.

[13]Ibid., pp. 25–26.

San Antonio, Atlanta, Milwaukee (Again), and Elsewhere

Private vouchers have spread from Indianapolis to San Antonio, Atlanta, Little Rock, and even Milwaukee. In San Antonio, the Children's Educational Opportunity (CEO) Foundation has awarded 929 scholarships and has over 1,000 students on the waiting list. Patricia Farnan tells of one nearly desperate mother whose children were saved by the San Antonio program:

> Etta Wallace, mother of three boys now attending St. Mary Magdalene school in San Antonio, explained that she was tired of her children being attacked and beaten by gang members at the public school. "When I tried to transfer the children the school blamed my boys for the trouble. After many incidents, they finally transferred them to a school far from my home with the same gang problems as the school they just left. When I learned about the CEO Foundation program I was so relieved. Now they attend St. Mary Magdalene school and I have yet to be called for a single incident. The boys' grades are improving, and they are much happier in their new school."[14]

How do parents feel about the voucher programs? In Atlanta, when the Children's Education Foundation offered private scholarship vouchers, 5,500 people applied within nine days. In Milwaukee, the state-funded program sponsored by Polly Williams is limited by law to fewer than 1,000 students, but Partners Advancing Values in Education provides privately funded half-tuition vouchers to 2,146 more. Those students attend 85 different schools. Another 900 students on the waiting list. Additional private voucher programs are being established in Arizona, California, Florida, Maryland, New York, and Washington, D.C.[15]

Cambridge, Massachusetts

Some jurisdictions, while eschewing independent school choice, at least allow parents to choose from among the government schools. One such "controlled choice" program began in Cambridge, Massachusetts, in 1981. Desegregation attempts based on magnet schools, redrawn boundaries, and forced busing were failing. The ordinary

[14]Ibid., p. 26.
[15]Ibid., pp. 26–27.

pattern in such circumstances is discouraging: the school district uses more and more money trying to force people to go where they don't want to go, academic achievement is all but forgotten, and racial balance becomes ever more unattainable as whites flee the deteriorating schools.

To its credit, the Cambridge district boldly tried something different: it let go. Rather than forcing students to go where the district wanted them, the district let students go where their parents wanted them. A Parent Information Center explains the features of the district's various schools. Parents and students may list up to four schools on their applications. The district considers several factors, including sibling attendance and racial balance, in assigning students to schools. The majority of students go to their first choice; nearly all students end up attending one of their top four choices.

The results? John Chubb and Terry Moe report "a huge improvement over the district's troubled past," with gains in both racial balance and student achievement. Parents, teachers, and students all seem more satisfied with the schools. Most impressively of all, the government schools are increasing their market share—from 78 percent of kindergarten students in 1979 to 89 percent in 1987. Chubb and Moe call this "the most concrete of all measures of success: people are choosing public schools because they prefer them."[16]

East Harlem, New York

Another bold and successful example of government school choice is Manhattan's District No. 4 in East Harlem, New York. Over half the district's families are headed by single females. Of the 14,000 students, 60 percent are Hispanic, 35 percent are black, and 80 percent qualify for the free lunch program. In 1973, of New York City's 32 school districts, District No. 4 ranked last in reading and math scores. Rather than simply demanding more tax money to do more of the same, District No. 4, like Cambridge, tried something different. Beginning in 1974, district leaders fostered the creation of alternative schools, each with its own distinctive mission. Where did these schools come from? Chubb and Moe tell the exciting story:

[16]John E. Chubb and Terry M. Moe, *Politics, Markets and America's Schools* (Washington: Brookings Institution, 1990), pp. 210–12. See also Robert S. Peterkin, "Choice and Change in Public Schools," in *Liberating Schools: Education in the Inner City*, ed. David Boaz (Washington: Cato Institute, 1991), pp. 173–79.

The district encouraged teachers with ideas and initiative to put forward their own proposals, and, with the district's involvement and consent, form their own schools. Teachers were only too happy to take advantage of these opportunities, and schools sprouted up like mushrooms.[17]

Conventional educrats think the only way to open a new school is to spend several years and millions of dollars erecting a new building. But for District No. 4, "school" is no longer synonymous with "building." Some district properties host several schools, each with its own teacher-director, and each with substantial autonomy. The individual schools even get to control their own admissions. Such freedom frightens opponents of California's Parental Choice in Education Initiative, who predict massive dislocations as autonomous schools, government and independent, reject all but the best students. The experience of District No. 4 shows such fears to be unfounded:

Freeing up the supply and governance of schools has not led to the kind of chaos or unfairness that critics of market arrangements invariably predict. The system appears to work smoothly, effectively, and fairly. While schools have control over their own admissions, their distinctiveness and their sheer need for students—the district puts them out of business if they fail to attract enough clients—has meant that schools and students tend to match up quite well on their own. In recent years, 60 percent of the students have received their first choices, 30 percent their second choices, and 5 percent their third choices.[18]

Results? Teachers are enthusiastic; parents are active in the schools and take pride in them; and student achievement is way up. By 1987, District No. 4 had moved from last place among New York districts to the middle. In 1973, 15.9 percent of the district's students were reading at grade level. By 1987, 62.6 percent were doing so.[19]

---

[17]Chubb and Moe, p. 212. See also Seymour Fliegel, *Miracle in East Harlem* (New York: Times Books, 1993).

[18]Chubb and Moe, pp. 213–14.

[19]Ibid., pp. 214–15.

Higher Education

Despite the success of parental choice wherever and to whatever degree it is allowed, it is anathema to the education establishment and thus rare in America's government school system. Yet free choice is the rule in American higher education. Is it coincidental that our system of higher education is considered the best in the world? Nobel laureate Milton Friedman, for one, thinks not:

> Suppose you go around the world, any country you want to, and ask the following two questions. First, what country leads the world in higher education, in colleges and universities? Wherever you go around the world, you will get the same answer: the United States. We are the magnet for people from around the world who want to go to colleges and universities. . . .
>
> Now suppose you go around the world and ask exactly the same question about elementary and secondary schools. There will not be a single person around the world who will list the United States as a leader. We are first class in higher education; we are third class in elementary and secondary schooling. Isn't that a paradox?
>
> Why is it that we are world class on one level and third class on another level? For exactly the same reason that the Soviet Union is a disaster and the United States is an affluent country. At the higher level you have competition.[20]

If I want to go to college, any state or federal government aid for which I qualify—Pell grants, guaranteed student loans, GI bill assistance, or other—will follow me to the college of my choice, whether it is a public, private, or parochial institution. Financial aid is not restricted to those attending public colleges. Nobody is compelled to attend any particular college, so the colleges all compete for students, and the students choose freely among them. The result? According to dozens of experts, both American and foreign, "Americans have the most successful system of higher education," bar none.[21]

---

[20]Milton Friedman, "The California Parental Choice Initiative." Speech presented at the conference on "Rebuilding California's Schools: The Educational Choice Debate," May 1, 1992, Pacific Research Institute for Public Policy, San Francisco.

[21]"The Best Schools in the World," *Newsweek*, December 2, 1991, p. 51.

Imagine what would happen if we operated our system of higher education the way we operate K–12 education. Ignoring the educational interests of individual students and the educational offerings of the various colleges, we would simply require all college students to attend the state-funded college or university nearest them. Aggrieved students could petition for transfer, but either the original college or the desired one could deny the request. We would prevent college students from using state financial aid to attend any private university; thus only the wealthiest students could consider doing so.

Does anyone seriously think that would improve higher education? Of course not, but that is the way we run our government schools. School choice simply extends to elementary and secondary education the system that already works so well for higher education. It allows parents to choose freely among government and independent schools. State aid follows the student to the chosen school. It is simple, proven, and fair.

Supply, Demand, and Continuing Improvement

Chapter 5 described the Lincoln Alternative School in Corona, California, where parents camp out in the parking lot all weekend hoping to be able to enroll their children. It is not an isolated phenomenon. Around the country, whenever a government school district opens an alternative school focusing on the basics, parents wait in lines for hours to get their kids in. Given even a sliver of choice, parents grasp it.

One wishes that school districts would respond by creating more of the schools parents are clamoring for. Instead they do the opposite: rather than increasing the supply, they restrict the demand. One superintendent suggested assigning seats in the desirable schools by lottery. "Can one imagine a private firm responding to increased demand in such a way?" asks David Boaz. "The market is shouting, 'Make more schools like this,' and the suppliers respond by looking for new ways to ration access."[22] Bill Bennett tells of the "Innovative Skills School" ("innovative" because it emphasized reading, writing, arithmetic, and geography) in Arlington, Virginia. Parents were invited to apply to any of Arlington's government elementary

[22]David Boaz, "The Public School Monopoly: America's Berlin Wall," in *Liberating Schools: Education in the Inner City*, ed. David Boaz (Washington: Cato Institute, 1991), p. 29.

schools, but 85 percent of them applied to that one. Had they operated in a free market, the administrators would have converted the
other schools in a hurry if they wanted to stay in business. "Instead,"
reports Bennett, "they abolished the program. It was too disruptive.
It was drawing people away from the other schools."[23]

Consider how different things would be under school choice.
Under the present system, once the alternative school is full, parents
are out of luck. If district officials refuse to expand the program or
decide to abolish it, too bad. Under choice, parents can keep shopping. Perhaps there is a good independent school with a similar
curriculum; now they have a scholarship whose value is probably
more than enough to pay tuition for their child. Or perhaps a neigh-
boring government school district has a strong academic program;
if there is space, their child gets in. Meanwhile, the home district is
losing students. Under the current system, so what? Under school
choice, the administrators had better figure out why students are
leaving and do something to make them want to stay, or the administrators will soon be administrating an empty school with an empty
budget. That focuses the attention. Out of self-preservation if for no
other reason, school officials will be forced to emulate the qualities
of the good schools that are drawing students away.

Thus, parental choice drives continuing improvement; it keeps
the system on its toes. It forces school officials to pay attention to
what is working elsewhere and to do it. It promotes innovation. It
gives parents consumer power, so schools have to satisfy the customer. Unlike conventional school reforms, which require massive
political energy to enact and implement and are then locked into
the massive Education Code, parental choice creates a fluid, dynamic
system responding in countless small ways to countless small inputs.
It turns a top-down, command-and-control, one-size-fits-all, Civil
War–era hierarchy into a bottom-up, free-market, infinitely diverse,
information age network.

Liberation

School choice puts parents squarely in control of the education
of their children. It promises to dramatically improve the quality of

[23]William J. Bennett, "An Obligation to Educate," *California Political Review*, Summer
1992, p. 21.

education by giving schools strong incentives to please parents and by giving parents complete freedom to choose among competing schools. It promises to liberate teachers, principals, and schools. As Chubb and Moe note,

> Because education is based on personal relationships and interactions, on continual feedback, and on the knowledge, skills, and experience of teachers, most of the necessary technology and resources are inherently present in the school itself. . . . Higher-level administrative units have little to contribute that is not already there.[24]

Those higher-level administrative units are there in response to political pressures; they have little to do with educating children. A system based on parental choice will favor schools that devote resources to their classrooms instead of their supervising bureaucracies.

Where government and independent school administrative practices differ, school choice will let parents determine for themselves which results in a better education. For example, an independent school principal is usually free to

> systematically recruit the kinds of teachers he wants and weed out those he does not, giving weight to whatever qualifications have a direct bearing on organizational performance, regardless of how intangible or resistant to formalization they might be. Through this selection process, principals are in a position to create and maintain what can meaningfully be called a team—a group of teachers whose values, talents, backgrounds, and personalities mesh well together and promote the cooperative pursuit of organizational objectives.[25]

If such an approach creates a more desirable school, government school districts would have to decentralize personnel decisions and give similar authority to their principals in order to compete. The teachers unions would, of course, object to such reforms, but

> unions operate at a serious disadvantage in a market setting. Teachers who are team players, who have lots of autonomy

[24]Chubb and Moe, p. 36.
[25]Ibid., pp. 51–52.

in their work, who routinely play integral roles in school decisionmaking, and who are treated as professionals are hardly good candidates for union membership. They are likely to be happy with their situations. . . . Unions do best in noncompetitive, protected, regulated settings—like government—where costs can simply be passed on and ineffectiveness has almost nothing to do with organizational survival.[26]

Why Choice Works

On its face, the Parental Choice in Education Initiative neither favors nor disfavors particular methods of school management. It does not attempt to define what a good education is or how it may be obtained. All it does is give each parent the power to make such determinations for him or herself, and the ability to choose accordingly. But what a difference that simple change will make!

Wherever parents have been given free choice of schools—including Milwaukee, Indianapolis, San Antonio, Atlanta, Cambridge, East Harlem, and districts nationwide offering alternative schools—they have exercised it enthusiastically and wisely. Wherever schools have had to compete with each other for students—as in American higher education—quality is high. Competition breeds excellence. Compulsion breeds resentment. The government school system with which we are presently saddled relies on compulsion, not free choice; on control, not free competition. Switch those elements and remarkable, even miraculous, things happen. Formerly apathetic low-income parents in Milwaukee, who never attended government school meetings, turn out in droves to win the right to choose schools for themselves. District No. 4 in East Harlem breaks the mold and shows dramatic academic improvement. Students who fled the Cambridge government schools start coming back of their own accord.

By replacing compulsion with competition, school choice makes the schools far more responsive to individual needs and desires, and it gives both parents and students a sense of ownership, of

[26]Ibid., p. 53.

investment, in their schools.[27] It depoliticizes the schools. In politics, one side wins and one side loses, and the winners get to set the policy. In a free market, each participant's needs can be met in different ways, and nobody gets to set policy for anyone else.

"If you want to buy an automobile," says Milton Friedman, "you won't find a shortage, but if you try to find a place to drive it you might. That is because highways are provided by the government and the cars are provided by private enterprise."[28] There is no shortage of children, but there is a pronounced shortage of good schools for them. That doesn't need to be.

---

[27]An example: In Chapter 2 we reviewed the debate over condom distribution in the Los Angeles Unified School District (LAUSD). The forces favoring condom distribution won, so condoms are now available in all LAUSD high schools. But why should such matters be decided by a school board with only one member for every 90,000 students? Why not let parents who want condoms distributed put their children in schools that do so, and parents who object put their children in schools that do not? Under the initiative, parents can choose for themselves; such contentious issues will tend to be decided school by school, rather than by a political body whose decision binds all. If sweeping political decisions are still imposed, the initiative offers alternatives.

[28]Friedman.

11. Making It Happen

"It's obvious that school choice is needed," a friend of mine once said, "but do you really think it will ever pass?" In the wake of the defeat of Proposition 174, many others are asking the same question. Bombarded with anti-initiative propaganda purchased in part with tax dollars and distributed through the government schools, California parents in particular may be forgiven for despairing of ever changing the system. Those who hoped for success in Oregon, then Colorado, then California, may be forgiven some discouragement.

Yet the long-term prospects for school choice are good. Proponents have history and human nature on their side, and they are fighting for a better cause. Socialism has failed around the world, and it is failing in the government school system. Freedom and choice work; compulsion and monopoly don't. The educrats aren't fighting to help children, but to save their own jobs. So obvious are the shortcomings, the injustices, and the expense of the present system, and so clear the benefits of allowing parental choice, that eventual implementation of something like the Parental Choice in Education Initiative is almost inevitable.

Polls taken early in the California campaign showed overwhelming public support for the initiative. The education establishment's negative campaign reversed that support, but it did nothing to improve the continuing poor performance of, or low public regard for, the government school system. Thus the issue of school choice will not go away. To most parents the education of their children matters more than any other political issue, and the government school system is not working well. The question is not whether we will have school choice, but when and how.

Recommendations

Perhaps proponents of school choice can hasten its acceptance and implementation by applying some of the lessons of the California campaign. As Chapter 9 notes, the defeat of Proposition 174 was due to a lopsided campaign, not textual or conceptual flaws. Nevertheless, a few modifications will improve the text considerably and make it less vulnerable to attack. The most effective attacks on the initiative focused on its fiscal impact and the purported danger of unregulated schools. These charges are spurious, of course; but the Parental Choice in Education Initiative can be amended to deter their reappearance and strengthen the case for school choice.

A Graduated Phase-In

The most obvious fiscal concern is the cost of awarding scholarships to students already attending independent schools. Paragraph (a)(5) states:

> **Children enrolled in private schools on October 1, 1991, shall receive scholarships, if otherwise eligible, beginning with the 1995–96 fiscal year. All other children shall receive scholarships beginning with the 1993–94 fiscal year.**[1]

In other words, government school students of all grade levels qualify for scholarships the year following the initiative's approval; independent school students qualify two years later. Proponents expected the savings from government school students after two years to match or outweigh the cost of including independent school students. Opponents, however, disagreed. The ensuing dispute over the initiative's precise fiscal impact generated more heat than light.

If I were rewriting the initiative for the 1996 ballot, I would replace the language of paragraph (a)(5) with the following:

> **Beginning with the school year immediately following approval of this initiative, scholarships shall be made available to every otherwise eligible child born on or after January 1, 1992.**

The program would begin in the 1997–98 school year with children aged five or younger. It would apply to those children as they progressed from kindergarten through 12th grade, and to all children following them. In the program's first year of operation most eligible students would be kindergartners; in the next year, kindergartners

---

[1] In practice, the effective dates would have been moved back one year each. See the analysis of this subsection in Chapter 6.

and first graders; in the following year, kindergartners, first graders, and second graders; and so on.

This 12-year phase-in makes fiscal projections much simpler. It also makes the fiscal impact easier to explain. Since current students of either government or independent schools are excluded, the only question is, how many entering kindergarten students will accept scholarships rather than attend a government school? Every one that does so saves the taxpayers $2,600. It is mathematically impossible to predict a negative fiscal impact.[2]

The extended phase-in process has other advantages, both practical and political. Since it progresses only one grade per school year, it permits a smooth transition from the current system. It gives the government school system ample time to adjust to a competitive environment and gives independent schools ample time to expand capacity. It also gives the state time to evaluate the program and adjust its budget and administrative mechanisms accordingly.

The obvious disadvantage of the extended phase-in is that whole generations of students would graduate without the opportunity to attend independent schools before the choice program became fully operational. Some proponents of school choice think that the extended phase-in gives away too much. They may be right, but I have yet to see a competing proposal of comparable clarity and simplicity that so effectively deals with concerns about the program's potential fiscal impact.

A possible middle ground would be a four-year phase-in, in which scholarship vouchers were offered to students in kindergarten through third grade in the first year, kindergarten through sixth grade in the second year, kindergarten through ninth grade in the third year; and kindergarten through twelfth grade in the fourth year and thereafter. But such a proposal would need to be accompanied by a highly credible independent economic analysis showing with substantial certainty that the program would impose no net new cost on the taxpayers in any given year.

School Accountability

By giving parents the right and the means to transfer their children to competing institutions, school choice makes all schools, both government and independent, immediately and directly accountable

---

[2]Unless, of course, one wildly exaggerates the administrative costs; but the California Legislative Analyst's Office estimated these at only $3 per student per year. One could also argue that the government schools' fixed costs remain constant even as

to parents. Notwithstanding that, opponents criticized the Parental Choice in Education Initiative for potentially allowing allegedly unregulated independent schools to redeem scholarships with minimal state oversight. The criticism was effective: exit polling showed that California voters wanted the initiative to impose more stringent controls over the quality of independent schools and teachers.

The purported concerns about quality are answered in Chapter 7. Future initiatives could blunt such criticism and assuage such concerns by imposing identical professional standards, performance measurements, and reporting requirements on government and scholarship-redeeming independent schools. But such provisions undercut the fundamental premises of school choice, which are that (1) parents are better supervisors of their children's education than are distant legislators and bureaucrats, and (2) freedom to respond to the needs and preferences of free citizens in a free market allows a better result than compelling compliance with centrally impose regulations. The real challenge isn't to draft a stricter initiative, but to run a more persuasive campaign.

Still, certain basic professional standards, performance measurements, and reporting requirements, *imposed on government and scholarship-redeeming independent schools alike,* could make the political dynamic more favorable for choice. Some possible provisions:

- Each school must make public its budget and the results of an annual independent audit.
- Each teacher must hold a college degree in the subject taught, have equivalent work experience, or pass a competency exam.
- Each student must be tested in particular academic subjects at specified grade levels. Test results by school, grade, and class must be made public.

Parental choice will do more to spur educational quality than any of these requirements. However, the education establishment has more to fear from them than do the independent schools! Thus, such requirements may put the government schools system on the defensive and help persuade voters to give choice a chance. Most independent schools would not object. "Accountability is no problem at all," said Joseph McElligott, associate director for education

---

enrollment declines. Given California's burgeoning enrollment, however, such an argument is purely hypothetical.

of the California Catholic Conference. "Eighty-five percent of all Catholic school teachers already hold California credentials."[3]

Future initiatives might be able to minimize concern over independent school quality without imposing any new requirements at all. Numerous state laws and regulations already govern independent schools and teachers. Simply restating them in future initiatives would make no difference in independent schools' operation but could make a considerable difference in public perception.

The Next Campaign

Proponents of Proposition 174 were fortunate, in one sense, that their opponents outspent them so greatly: it was a great excuse for losing. Yes on 174 needed more than another $14 million in the treasury to run a winning campaign. They needed a broad coalition, a clear and consistent message presented through appealing and simple themes, and an intelligent strategy and action plan for winning at least 50 percent of the votes. The opponents had all of those; Yes on 174 had none.

None of this should detract from the accomplishment of the handful of people who made it possible to put 174 on the ballot and mount the campaign. They never received the help they deserved from the business community and others who should have been their allies. Obviously with funding to match the opponents, it would have been easier for them to assemble a coalition, develop a message, and formulate and execute a strategy.

To succeed, future campaigns will need a much broader coalition that provides much better funding and presents a much clearer message. No exogenous force is going to level the playing field; those who believe in the promise of school choice need to work to build the critical mass necessary for a statewide initiative campaign or state legislation to succeed. It is time to develop alliances among business, taxpayer, and independent school associations; to establish private scholarship programs for low-income students in every major city; to implement pilot school choice programs on the local level. As with education, there is no one best system or one best way. The movement needs a variety of approaches to overcome the variety of obstacles blocking passage of school choice programs.

[3]Stephanie Chavez and Dan Morain, "Voucher Backers Vow to Continue Fight," *Los Angeles Times*, November 4, 1993, pp. A3, A37.

What the People Want

And those obstacles will be overcome. So far the education establishment has defeated school choice almost everywhere, which only serves to show that it cannot afford to lose anywhere. School choice movements are gathering force throughout the country. Despite the negative campaign in California, the concept of parental choice remains popular. Support for it transcends the usual political divisions. And why not? Why should we force any child to stay in a school that isn't working? Why shouldn't parents be allowed to choose the school that best meets their child's needs?

The Milwaukee school choice program enjoys 59 percent support among the general population and 83 percent support among African-Americans.[4] Similar support exists nationwide. In an NBC News–*Wall Street Journal* survey conducted in May 1991, 56 percent of likely voters supported giving parents tax credits or vouchers for the government or independent school of their choice; only 36 percent opposed the idea. The strongest supporters were African-Americans and blue-collar workers.[5] In a July 1992 Gallup poll, support had risen to 70 percent. School choice was favored by almost every demographic group surveyed, including 84 percent of Hispanics and 86 percent of blacks. Asked explicitly whether they favored releasing some tax money currently given to government schools and using it to enable children to attend the government, private, or parochial school of their choice, 61% said yes.[6] In September 1992, an Associated Press survey showed that 63 percent of voters supported President Bush's school choice plan, the "G.I. Bill for Kids," and a Lou Harris poll showed that 69 percent of voters favored full public-private school choice, including vouchers.[7]

In Orange County, California, a June 1993 *Los Angeles Times* poll found that voters favored the Parental Choice in Education Initiative by a two-to-one ratio. Absolutely every demographic group surveyed favored the initiative. The majority of Republicans favored

[4]"Choice Facts," *Wall Street Journal*, February 6, 1992, reporting results of a Gordon Black poll sponsored by the Wisconsin Policy Research Institute.

[5]Diana Walsh, "Push for School Vouchers," *San Francisco Examiner*, January 21, 1992, p. A-1.

[6]"Poll Says 70% of Americans Support School Vouchers," *Los Angeles Times*, September 19, 1992, p. B5.

[7]"Choice Landslide," *Wall Street Journal*, September 21, 1992, p. A10.

it—as did the majority of Democrats. The majority of parents with children at home favored it—as did the majority of other voters. Raising taxes to increase government school funding, in contrast, did not receive majority support, perhaps because only 37 percent of parents with children in government schools wanted to keep them there.[8]

Among the parents interviewed in the *Times* poll was Julie Barrientes of Irvine, a Democrat. She and her husband both work full time and earn a combined income of under $50,000. They want to enroll their son in a Catholic school but cannot afford it. With the initiative's scholarship, they could and would. Other families she knows would also choose independent schools if they could afford to. Asked about the impact on government schools, Barrientes replied, "I'm not going to let my son suffer if I can help it, just because I don't want the public school system to go down the drain."[9]

Adela de la Torre writes of her mother's "agonizing emotional and financial choice" to send her to a parochial school. She asked her mother—a single parent and a government schoolteacher—why she couldn't attend the government school with her friends. Her mother replied, "You were the only children I would have in my lifetime and I was unwilling to sacrifice you for any cause, even a cause I believe in."[10]

More and more parents are coming to the same conclusion as Julie Barrientes and Adela de la Torre's mother. They are unwilling to sacrifice their children to "the one best system" when alternatives are so obviously preferable. "A generation that viewed itself as open-minded and socially committed," writes Elizabeth Shogren, is suffering "a humbling showdown with conscience as it abandons the public school system." She reports that, just like President Clinton, politically liberal baby boomers around the country are concluding that they cannot consign their own children to the neighborhood government schools.[11]

[8]Dave Lesher and Nancy Wride, "Voucher Plan Gets High Marks," *Los Angeles Times*, June 13, 1993, p. A1.

[9]Ibid., pp. A1, A30.

[10]Adela de la Torre, "Voucher Opponents Miss the Point," *Los Angeles Times*, October 20, 1993, p. B9 (Orange County edition).

[11]Elizabeth Shogren, "A Private Dilemma for Parents," *Los Angeles Times*, January 26, 1993, p. A1.

They don't need to feel guilty—if they are willing to extend the same choice to all parents. Barbara Reynolds writes:

> After a PTA meeting at my son's public elementary school, I overheard two of his teachers sharing stories about their kids in private schools.
>
> As soon as I could, I angrily snatched my son out of the school. If the school wasn't good enough for their kids, my little darling wasn't going there either.
>
> I suspect such hypocrisy is common around the nation. And it's probably just as common among city-dwelling editors who endorse public education but send their kids to private schools.
>
> If they and the president's daughter can have school choice, why should the poor be denied that freedom? . . .
>
> California's Proposition 174 lost badly, but the core idea is not a loser.[12]

Some voters remember good experiences in the government schools of a generation or two ago, and they retain a residual reverence for the system. Others consider the government schools the common denominator of our common culture. But these views can change. As Jackie Ducote writes:

> I once thought giving parents vouchers was un-American because I had an almost religious attachment to the present system. Then . . . I started looking at public education in terms of what is best for children, not what is best for the education bureaucracy. Public education is a public service, but there is nothing that says the government has to be the sole provider of that service. Why should children be held captive in government institutions that are failing to educate them?[13]

The Failure of Socialism

In 1980 when I was first old enough to vote, I bought a book called *Can Capitalism Survive?*[14] It was not a rhetorical question. The

[12]Barbara Reynolds, "School-Choice Plans Give the Poor a Voice in Education," *USA Today*, November 5, 1993, p. 13A.

[13]Jackie Ducote, "Confessions of an Education-Reform Junkie," *Wall Street Journal*, December 14, 1990.

[14]Benjamin A. Rogge, *Can Capitalism Survive?* (Indianapolis: Liberty Press, 1979). The question was posed by Joseph Schumpeter in *Capitalism, Socialism, and Democracy* (New York: HarperCollins, 1962).

Soviet Union had recently invaded Afghanistan and was on its way to exterminating or banishing one of every four Afghans. The rampant brutality there was echoed in a growing number of totalitarian client states around the world. Shortly thereafter, under Soviet direction, the communist government of Poland tried to crush the Solidarity movement, jailing its leader, Lech Walesa. Throughout what was then called the Eastern bloc, political dissent was relentlessly suppressed, and those who dared speak freely—among them Czechoslovakia's greatest playwright, Vaclav Havel—were jailed, placed under house arrest, or forbidden to travel, publish, and even speak.

Who, back then, would have dared to predict that in little more than a decade, Vaclav Havel would lead the Czech Republic; that Lech Walesa would be president of an independent and free Poland; and that the once mighty Soviet Union would have already disappeared into the history books? Those of us fortunate enough to live during the 1980s and 1990s have witnessed a momentous phase of world history. It has some lessons to teach us. Among them are these, in the words of Warren Brookes, James Pinkerton, and Benno Schmidt, respectively:

> Socialist systems fail not only because they fail to energize the most productive asset of all, the individual human mind, but because as entrenched monopolies they are so totally unaccountable to the individual consumer—because they provide no market in which competing ideas and products can be tested, priced, approved or rejected, modified or abandoned.[15]
>
> The 1980s were a terrible decade for centralized bureaucracies and the people who depend on them—whether in the Soviet Union, New York City or General Motors.[16]
>
> The world has been revolutionized in recent years by the demand for freedom and choice, as concentrated political and economic power has given way to democratic governance and private ordering. Competition, freedom of opportunity and diversity serve the causes of progress and human

---

[15]Warren T. Brookes, "Public Education and the Global Failure of Socialism," *Imprimis*, April 1990, p. 4.

[16]James P. Pinkerton, quoted in Ronald Brownstein, "Reformers' Influence over GOP Is Growing," *Los Angeles Times*, August 20, 1992, p. A5.

dignity. These lessons have a profound bearing on American education, if we will but heed them.[17]

The opponents of school choice are on the losing side of history. Now that the blessings of freedom are available to the nations of Eastern Europe and the former Soviet empire, it is time to extend them to America's school-age children and their parents. "The collapse of the Iron Curtain may bring East Europeans not only freedoms long cherished by Americans but ones we don't enjoy yet," editorializes the *Wall Street Journal*. It writes of Poland's education reforms:

> It's no surprise that the Solidarity government lifted restrictions on private schools in 1990. What is remarkable is that it also concluded that the hidebound educational bureaucracy could be reformed only if it faced effective competition from private schools. . . . Parliament [passed] a law giving civic organizations and individuals the right to start private schools and be reimbursed for up to 50% of what it would have cost the state to educate their students.[18]

On a visit to the United States, Katarzyna Skorzynska, head of Poland's Office of Innovation and Independent Schools, said: "You have the same people who oppose choice as in my country: the trade unions and the education bureaucrats. The difference is that in my country their failures have completely discredited those groups."[19]

In Sweden, once the prototype of the welfare state, a new government announced a bold free-market reform agenda. The free market reforms extend to government education, as the *Wall Street Journal* reports:

> Government education money will go to individual students instead of schools, allowing parents the freedom to send their children to any private or public school. "Free competition will provide better value for the money spent, increase the role of parents in education and lead to more innovation,"

---

[17]Benno C. Schmidt, "Educational Innovation for Profit," *Wall Street Journal*, June 5, 1992, p. A12.

[18]"Poland's Liberated Schools," *Wall Street Journal*, January 7, 1992, p. A10.

[19]Ibid.

says [Sweden's education minister Beatrice] Ask. She is a fan
of Poland's educational reforms.[20]

The Promise of Freedom

What has begun to happen in Poland, Sweden, and a handful of
American cities should happen everywhere. It is time for a free
market in education. As John Taylor Gatto urges, "Give families
back their tax money to pick and choose—who could possibly be a
better shopper if the means for comparison were made available?
... Trust in families and neighborhoods and individuals to make
sense of the important question, 'What is education *for*?'"[21] That is
simply common sense, and it is an idea whose time has come. The
principles of individual liberty, private property, open markets, and
free competition are being embraced around the world. It is time to
apply them to the schools. School choice transcends the usual divisions of ideology, race, income, and party. It opens a way for all
students, including those from the poorest and most disadvantaged
families, to receive a better education. It expands the educational
opportunities available to all children dramatically.

Of course, school choice faces intense opposition from those with
a vested interest in maintaining the status quo. But the education
establishment opposes the initiative for reasons unrelated to its merits. They are afraid—not of its potential failure but of its certain
success. "In one of the great ironies of human affairs," writes Gatto,
"the massive rethinking the schools require would cost so much *less*
than we are spending now that powerful interests cannot afford to
let it happen."[22]

But it must happen. There is no alternative. Without competition
and freedom of choice, the government school system will continue
taking more and more money to produce less and less satisfactory
results. Thanks to the defeat of Proposition 174, California's school
system is on a collision course with reality. Statewide government
school enrollment is projected to increase from 5.2 million in 1992
to over 7.1 million in 2001.[23] Simply building schools for this tidal

[20]"The Swedish Model," *Wall Street Journal*, April 7, 1992, p. A16; and David Boaz,
"U.S. School Reform Lagging," *(Portland) Oregonian*, November 24, 1992, p. B5.

[21]John Taylor Gatto, *Dumbing Us Down* (Philadelphia: New Society Publishers,
1992), p. 103.

[22]Ibid., p. 19.

[23]Source: California Department of Finance projections.

wave of new students will cost $20 to $30 billion, and operating them will cost billions more. At those rates of growth, notes former assemblyman Tom McClintock, Proposition 98, the school-funding guarantee, "will ratchet up to consume the entire state budget within 20 years. California has come face to face with the reality that you can't continue to spend more than you take in."[24]

Through school choice we can afford to provide a better education for those two million new children and their counterparts throughout the country. They are our neighbors and our fellow citizens. We want them to be free to go as far as their abilities and industry will take them. Under the current system, they are not. We know we can do better; examples of excellent schools are all around us. But the present system reacts to them sluggishly, if at all, and seems more interested in excuses than in improvement.

Things will change. You can help make it happen.

[24]Assemblyman Tom McClintock, in a personal conversation on September 1, 1992.

Acknowledgments

This book grew out of my participation in drafting and promoting California's Parental Choice in Education Initiative. I thank all who helped create the initiative, qualify it for the ballot, and prepare this book for publication.

Drafting the Initiative

Joseph F. Alibrandi, chairman and chief executive officer of the Whittaker Corporation and former chairman of the California Business Roundtable's Education Task Force, led the effort to conceive the initiative, qualify it for the ballot, and mount a statewide campaign. With the help of Kevin Teasley, Alibrandi assembled a working group that considered possible initiative provisions. This group included Democrats, Republicans, Libertarians, and independents; members of public school boards and private school associations; prosperous entrepreneurs and residents of the inner city. Diverse in race, gender, background, and expertise, these individuals shared a common determination to make quality education available to every California child.

The working group reviewed several then-existing proposals before deciding that a new initiative was necessary. J. G. Ford incorporated the group's general recommendations into a draft "California School Choices Initiative" and circulated it for comment. David Barulich, Dr. Stephen Guffanti, and Andrew Paterson, among others, made substantial contributions.

Late in the summer of 1991, Alibrandi asked me to assess the legal and political acceptability of the resulting document and put it into proper form. This charge soon grew to encompass a complete rewriting of the initiative. Through September, October, and November of 1991, with the constant guidance of Manuel S. Klausner, I coordinated background legal research and the final drafting of the initiative. Thirteen successive drafts, each incorporating substantial

189

revisions, were sent to interested parties throughout the country. Suggestions from William Ball, Clint Bolick, Milton Friedman, State Senator Bill Leonard, and Myron Lieberman proved helpful. Attorneys in federal and state governments, public interest firms, private practice, and academia submitted useful revisions and additions. Blake Ashley, Stephen L. S. Davis, Don Franzen, Tom Hungar, Manny Klausner, John Lucas, and Shawn Steel deserve recognition for their volunteer legal work.

Drawing on the work of all these contributors, I wrote each successive draft of the Parental Choice in Education Initiative. On November 19, 1991, I wrote the final text. While I am responsible for the initiative's structure and much of its language, many concepts, clauses, and phrases came directly from other participants. The initiative represents a team effort.

The Qualification Campaign

To qualify the initiative for the ballot, the Excellence through Choice in Education League (ExCEL) had to obtain nearly one million voter signatures. Each of my colleagues on the board of directors devoted considerable time to the qualification effort. Former secretary of education William J. Bennett, former governor George Deukmejian, Nobel laureate Milton Friedman, former U.S. senator John Tunney, and Wisconsin state representative Polly Williams lent their expertise and prestige to our effort. Key contributors included Howard Ahmanson, Joe Alibrandi, Ev Berg, Ron Cedillos, Rich Dennis, Sam Hardage, Rob Hurtt, Bill Huston, Dr. Joe Jacobs, David Koch, Safi Qureshey, and Rich Snyder. Kevin Teasley coordinated campaign operations and fundraising. Steve Guffanti organized volunteers. Kay Torrans, Lyman Dennis, and Anne MacLellan led unusually effective volunteer signature-gathering efforts. David Barulich did the fiscal impact analysis and other research. The indefatigable Shawn Steel served as treasurer and the irrepressible Manny Klausner served as legal counsel. Volunteers, donors, and allies too numerous to mention also merit thanks.

The Book

Several people suggested that I write this book, but Jesse Riddle insisted that I do so. His persistent encouragement motivated me to start. David Barulich critiqued early drafts; the book is better for his editing. John Kurzweil gave a kind and helpful review. David Boaz took what I thought was the final manuscript and improved it. I thank each of them.

Most important, for so patiently enduring her quasi-single status while I was researching and writing, I thank Elayne Wells Harmer, my wife and very best friend.

Index

193

About the Author

David Harmer was born in Glendale, California. His father, John, represented the 21st District in the California state senate. His mother, Carolyn, raised 10 children, then returned to teaching school.

David attended both public and private schools, graduating from Oakmont High School in Roseville, California, in 1979. In 1984 he graduated from Brigham Young University with a degree in English, after which he taught college English and guided whitewater rafting expeditions.

In 1988 he graduated from the J. Reuben Clark Law School at BYU. His legal experience includes government, public interest, and private practice. He has been counsel to a subcommittee of the U.S. Senate Judiciary Committee, a fellow of the College of Public Interest Law at Pacific Legal Foundation, and an associate in the Los Angeles–based law firm O'Melveny & Myers.

David Harmer coordinated the drafting of the Parental Choice in Education Initiative and served as president of ExCEL, the Excellence through Choice in Education League. He has promoted school choice in public speeches and television appearances throughout California and on radio broadcasts throughout the nation.

He now lives in Utah with his wife Elayne.

Cato Institute

Founded in 1977, the Cato Institute is a public policy research foundation dedicated to broadening the parameters of policy debate to allow consideration of more options that are consistent with the traditional American principles of limited government, individual liberty, and peace. To that end, the Institute strives to achieve greater involvement of the intelligent, concerned lay public in questions of policy and the proper role of government.

The Institute is named for *Cato's Letters*, libertarian pamphlets that were widely read in the American Colonies in the early 18th century and played a major role in laying the philosophical foundation for the American Revolution.

Despite the achievement of the nation's Founders, today virtually no aspect of life is free from government encroachment. A pervasive intolerance for individual rights is shown by government's arbitrary intrusions into private economic transactions and its disregard for civil liberties.

To counter that trend, the Cato Institute undertakes an extensive publications program that addresses the complete spectrum of policy issues. Books, monographs, and shorter studies are commissioned to examine the federal budget, Social Security, regulation, military spending, international trade, and myriad other issues. Major policy conferences are held throughout the year, from which papers are published thrice yearly in the *Cato Journal*. The Institute also publishes the quarterly magazine *Regulation*.

In order to maintain its independence, the Cato Institute accepts no government funding. Contributions are received from foundations, corporations, and individuals, and other revenue is generated from the sale of publications. The Institute is a nonprofit, tax-exempt, educational foundation under Section 501(c)3 of the Internal Revenue Code.

CATO INSTITUTE
1000 Massachusetts Ave., N.W.
Washington, D.C. 20001